D1610907

TAM: THE LIFE AND DEATH OF A DOG

For H.H.S.

TAM

THE LIFE AND DEATH OF A DOG

DEREK BOWMAN

Derek Bowman

GORDON WRIGHT PUBLISHING
55 MARCHMONT ROAD, EDINBURGH EH9 1HT
SCOTLAND

S.B.N. 903065 25 8

Photographs 1, 3, 7, 8 by Derek Bowman.
Photographs 2, 4, 5, 6 by Gordon Wright.

Printed in Scotland by
Macdonald Printers (Edinburgh) Limited
Edgefield Road, Loanhead, Midlothian

PART ONE

"Why should a dog, a horse, a rat,
have life . . . ?"
Shakespeare

1974

EDINBURGH: WEDNESDAY, 14 AUGUST

This morning I went with my brother John and sister-in-law Choni and their children, Marie and John Manuel, to Waverley Station to see them off on the London train. Elisabeth, 14 years old, and Catherine, 10, my daughters, came with me. On the way back we were walking up Cockburn Street—looks better than it did—when the girls said

"Why don't we just call in at the pet shop? Down the steps".

—Dead casual. So we did. Do anything to oblige, I will.

In we went. Sawdust on the floor, that stale animal smell, slightly sweet, like in a circus. Cages round the walls, most of them empty. In one at the far end, two little dogs, one jet-black, the other brindled black and white, stood there, shivering and whimpering sporadically. Brothers by the looks of them.

The girls made a bit of a fuss of them, well, you couldn't help it. Then didn't their little tails start wagging! Just as if a motor inside had been switched on. They put their faces to the mesh, falling over one another in their eagerness, and started licking our hands as best they could.

The girls and I were taken with the black one. Something about him. There he sat, small, chunky on his haunches, looking at us out of those great sad eyes as we finally left the shop.

"Nothing doing," I said to the girls.

Marianne, my wife, has said more than once that she's categorically opposed to having a dog in the house,

"It's either me or it. If a dog comes, I go! And that's flat!"

What could you do?

So we went home, talking about the dog the whole time.

"Well, no-one can stop you talking," said Elisabeth.

I couldn't get the black one out of my head, nor could the girls. Those eyes. We talked and talked about him over tea, trying, I suppose, to win Marianne over.

In the end she said "Alright then, as long as you do the dirty work. But I know how it'll work out, I'll end up feeding him, looking after him, and clearing up the mess. It's always the same".

"Oh, no!" came the chorus. So we decided to give him a try.

Not a bad day's work, eh?

THURSDAY, 15 AUGUST

This morning, as soon as they were open, Elisabeth rang up the pet shop. I could hear her there in the hall.

"Are the two 'collie crosses' " (that's what they called them) "still there?"

"No, one's gone."

(Breathless) "which one?"

"The brindled one."

"Thank goodness! Then you still have the black one?"

"Yes".

"We want to buy him. He's £2, isn't he?" (£2 for a dog, £1 for a bitch, males being less trouble.)

"Yes. I'll keep him till you come in. When will that be?"

"Right away."

Straight after breakfast (golloped down) the girls and I went in by the 41 bus and bought him. What would he need? For a start, at least for the first few weeks, the man said, he'd require twice a day, morning and evening, a feed of milk-saps. Thereupon he produced a thick fawn china bowl. Then he must have a lead, whereupon the man took one down. Identity disc—that was necessary too.

"And don't forget to get a license. See you get one by the end of the first six months. It doesn't cost much—37½p." And we were not to let him walk on the pavement till he'd had his injections.

"When should he get them?"

"After six weeks."

The pet-shop salesman lifted the dog—ours now—out of his cage, where he'd been standing disconsolately on his own, without his brother (they were both from the same litter, from down in the Borders) and handed him to me.

Once we were out of the shop, the girls took turns to carry him along the High Street. We even let him walk, or rather tumble along a bit. How bouncy he was, how frisky! People stopped to stroke him, or smiled as they walked past. How could you resist? A middle-aged worried-looking man in a suit took him up, cradled him in his arms and told us all about his own fox-terrier, Patsie.

What would we call him? On the bus going in, after several tries I hit on Tam, a good old Scottish name. The girls were all for it. So Tam it is.

You should have seen the little fellow, light as a feather, bouncing about the Meadows, by Jawbone Walk, when we at last let him down properly! From every move he made, from every ridiculous high-pitched yap it was obvious how glad he was to be out and about at last, and to *belong,* to be part of a family.

Marianne was out shopping when we got back, but she took to him right away. No bother.

FRIDAY, 16 AUGUST

Last night in his cardboard box there in the kitchen he cried and cried the whole night through, a continual high-pitched whimper, like a pram that needs oiling. No good shutting the door on him, that cry carried throughout the house. It was heart-breaking. Not only that, it's making us all irritable, we hardly got a wink of sleep. Over breakfast Marianne and I started snapping at the girls and Catherine started crying. Tam was moping in the kitchen. What have we let ourselves in for?

SATURDAY, 17 AUGUST

Tam a bit better during the day. He couldn't have been much worse. You should see him—the picture of misery in his cardboard box. Still subdued though, apart from piddling everywhere in the kitchen and hall when he does emerge. Still getting used to us, I suppose, and the house. It's been a big change for him.

How we dread the nights! We go to bed on tip-toe once he's quiet, but it's not long before the first whimper comes, then a long pause (we listen with bated breath—will it be the last?), then another whimper, then another, more and more frequent till the old crying's properly underway. It can go on for hours.

Marianne and I all on edge in bed upstairs. I said to her

"Perhaps it's the darkness in there."

I went down and put the light on. The crying stopped. I stayed a few minutes with Tam, stroking him, murmured endearments (you know the game). Tam quiet.

I close the kitchen door carefully, and am hardly up the stairs but he's at it again. So there's the four of us, all upset, jangled inside—for hours. What have we gone and done?

In the end—it must have been three o'clock by then—Marianne got up with a groan and an "I told you". I got up with her—well, it was the least I could do—and we went downstairs.

Marianne had a bright idea. She put the kettle on, filled one of our hot water bottles (Tam lying there in his box, watching her the whole time), put it in a piece of blanket, which she tied up with a safety pin and placed it in his box.

Well, he gave such a sigh, nestled up against it and—joy of joys!—closed his eyes.

I crept upstairs and whispered to the girls,

"Quick. Come and have a look."

There he lay, all small and round, coal-black against the fawn blanket, fast asleep at last.

"He must think it's his mother" said Marianne.

SUNDAY, 18 AUGUST

It's done the trick, just the odd whimper, otherwise Tam slept quite well, once he'd dropped off. After we'd duly made a fuss of him of course. What a relief!

The only trouble is, he wakes up so early and demands attention. And what a mess he makes everywhere! "Number 1 *and* number 2" said Catherine. "It's like having a baby all over again", said Marianne, "Only with him you can't use nappies".

I thought of how, when a baby gets a cold, you can't even blow its nose.

WEDNESDAY, 21 AUGUST

Still at it!—Piddles all over the floor and worse. Leaves his little pools and piles before we can get a newspaper under him. Papers everywhere, but it's almost as if he purposely avoids the ones we put down. Not that they smell—his piddles, I mean—but you can imagine Marianne's response, with *her* German upbringing.

What can you do, though, with such a baby? The trouble is, he's so friendly with it, comes up straight after for a cuddle. It's so difficult to resist him. And you can't hit him, not the size he is. But he's getting us down, one way and another. Talk about looming large! That such a wee body should cause such bother. Ridiculous, when you look at the size of him standing there. Why! he's hardly as big as my foot.

THURSDAY, 22 AUGUST

Margo, my cousin in Australia, is over on a visit to "the old country". She's staying with us for a few days, bringing her three year-old-daughter, Jenny, with her. I went down to the bus station at St Andrew's Square early this evening to pick them up—and us with our hands full like this. It never rains but it pours!

Nice to see them though. Margo hasn't changed a scrap.

FRIDAY, 23 AUGUST

Tam resumed his sporadic crying last night. Whenever he starts up, Marianne and I are on edge, there in bed, hoping it'll die down, whispering about him, thinking of our guests. He started up at half-five this morning! but it's no joke, he's wearing us out. Even the girls agree it can't go on like this.

WE'VE DECIDED TO PUT AN ADVERT IN THE "EVENING NEWS".

SATURDAY, 24 AUGUST

This morning, first thing after breakfast, I went into town, and handed in the advert at the "Scotsman and Evening News" offices. Mixed feelings, but what can you do?

It reads:

"Black labrador-collie-cross. Male. Six weeks old.

Free to a good home."

And I gave our home telephone-number.

SUNDAY, 25 AUGUST

I'm having second thoughts. All through Church this morning, I couldn't get Tam out of my head. Mind you, there wasn't much competition. That choir, and what a sermon! Fancy a grown-up clergyman blowing bubbles from a pulpit. I'm not kidding. Honestly!, we may need to become like little children, but there *are* limits. And then I kept hearing noises—that dry clicking of handbag after handbag before the collection, and the central heating clanking away, and me thinking the whole time, have we really done the right thing?

Margo, Marianne and I sat up talking till well past midnight. Hardly had Margo gone to bed, when Marianne says to me,

"Derek, I've something to tell you."

"Mm?"

"I've been wondering, have we been too hasty? You don't know where he might land up. We can't just *dump* him."

"I thought you couldn't wait to see the back of him."

"Yes, well. There have been times. You wanted to get rid of him yourself. Go on, admit it."

"Yes."

"Don't just say 'yes'. Tell me what you really think?"

"What *I* think? I say, let's give the boy another chance. We won't get another like him so easily."

"All right."

So the big decision made, we can at last go to bed.

Tam quiet.

MONDAY, 26 AUGUST

All those phone-calls, a score at least, from eight o'clock on. So many people anxious to take the dog "off our hands". Had to keep saying he'd already gone.

Later in the morning, went in to the David Hume Tower to see if there were any letters for me. Hardly arrived, when the elderly servitor at the counter says, right!, he'd take Tam. He and his wife had talked the matter over, they'd be glad to give him a good home.

I felt a right fool, saying I'd changed my mind. What a look he gave me!

SUNDAY, 1 SEPTEMBER

Marianne in her good grey suit, with the girls and me in town after lunch. Marianne's carrying Tam along Princes Street Gardens in her arms (he hasn't had his injections yet).

It's the height of the Festival, visitors everywhere, as well as the locals, all the people turning and smiling.

We sat down on the slope to listen to some execrable hymn-singing perpetrated by a band of middle-aged women in white gowns. Not far away, a big Airedale slowly goes down the slope to a deck chair where a man's raincoat is hanging, cocks its leg, and thoughtfully pees on it, then, with a serious face, gives it a good sniff before walking away. The man turns round and realises. All good clean fun! We turn past the giant silver thistles, then up the steps to the monument at the top—some chap on a horse. I rather like the seats gifted along Princes Street—nice gesture really—but you can have too many war-memorials, I say.

WEDNESDAY, 18 SEPTEMBER

Today Catherine bought a present for Tam from Dofo's, the pet shop along Morningside Road—and with her own money too.

It's a little red plastic barrel of the Watney's beer variety, to be hung from his collar. In it there's a roll of paper, like the ones bearing mottoes in Christmas crackers, with a space for his name and address. She's filled it in in her best handwriting.

Hanging there, it contrasts beautifully with his woolly black coat. He has just this tiny patch of white on his breast, otherwise he's as black as your hat. His hair is as soft to the touch as the head of a dandelion.

THURSDAY, 3 OCTOBER

A dull day. Took Tam to the "Dick Vet" on the corner of the Meadows this morning, to get his first injections.

Walking under the trees, opposite the swings, some woman in a long filthy mac tied with string, holding two whippets on ropes, stops me and says, "Whatever you do, don't let him down on the Meadows. It's a hot-bed of infection. Deadly!" And me the world's worst hypochondriac, as it is. I can feel the miasma coming up at me from all the worn patches of soil. Talk about King Lear and his "blasts and fogs upon thee!"

Well, "the boy" was as good as gold when the moment came. How small he looked, standing there on the table! Not a murmur as the vet in his white overall held him and punctured his leg, not once but a few times. Apparently they're against distemper (I keep on calling it "dysentry"), hard-pad and all sorts of things. Oh yes, he had to be vaccinated as well. His inoculation certificate's amongst my papers upstairs. Must get a folder for him.

The great thing is he can now trot along the pavement, at last!, with the best of them.

FRIDAY, 4 OCTOBER

When I got back from the University, took Tam into Morningside, to the shops and back. Bouncing along there as large as life. Pausing at the odd gate, looking in, then glancing up at me, and continuing his trot. I felt quite proud.

What a splendid little fellow he is!—short fat legs, chunky body, square head (a bit on the large side), stump of black tail. Not a great yapper really. When he does, it's so high-pitched it's ridiculous.

How long ago is it now since we got him? Seven weeks? I can't believe it. How on earth did we exist without him?

FRIDAY, 11 OCTOBER

A great day!—Tam at last house-trained. Well, virtually. What a business! Best not go into all the unsavoury details. A few times though, we thought he'd never get the message.

He calls us now at 7 a.m. sharp. Really, he ought to be let out first thing, as he still has difficulty controlling his young bladder. You can tell he tries, but he will persist in spoiling things by lying on his back as soon as you come down, wanting his tummy to be rubbed, with his pee busy spurting out driblets right, left and centre. At all costs, though, he has to go through this affectionate ritual first. Touching really, as he must realise a wet floor can upset us. Then he shoots off to stand there at the back door, little pipsqueak that he is, wagging his stump, then jumping up, looking up at me, pleading to be let out, so eager to please, just like a child, a two-year-old, which I suppose he is when you come to think about it.

He still has the odd lapse, as I say, but that can happen to anyone. The great thing is the will's there, and where there's a will etc. etc.

13

SATURDAY, 12 OCTOBER

He's most insistent at 7 am with his crying, which is quite understandable. Doesn't want to let us (and himself) down. Same during the day. We rouse the girls—they take it by turns to get up, one week on, one week off. Soon they should be getting up automatically, at least that's the theory.

How proud he is when he's been a "good boy", and how he hates to be told he's been "naughty"! Then that tail of his (it's beginning to get longer) fairly slumps.

SUNDAY, 13 OCTOBER

New complication. Clock put back last night. An hour's extra lie-in this morning, you think. The trouble is, Tam wakes up at his old time—now six o'clock!—and starts crying. First the odd little whimper with a long pause. You hope against.hope there won't be another. Then another. Then another, at shorter and shorter intervals. Lying there in bed, I think of Marianne's labour pains coming on when she had Elisabeth in Southampton years ago.

Now the crying's constant. Marianne nudges me (there's no need—I'm wide awake).

"Same with the girls" she says, "when the clock was put back, they still wanted their morning feed at the old time."

"I don't remember."

"No wonder! You used to sleep through it all. Well, what about it? You'd better get one of the girls up, hadn't you?"

Once he has an animal to look after it's not long before even an old spoilt urbanite like myself is made to realise the ancient rhythms of nature. Women have always known them.

I can see it'll take some time before Tam gets into a new routine.

TUESDAY, 5 NOVEMBER

Already you can see the sheep-dog coming out in him. Even at his age. The way he barks at Marianne's brush for instance, when she sweeps the path down the back garden. Gets quite fierce he does, snaps at it, trying to wrest it from her. He must think it's a sheep or a lamb that needs rounding up.

This afternoon, I got down on the green carpet in our front room and did a couple of rounds on all fours, bleating, just to test. Goodness me! You should have seen him. Talk about excited! For all his smallness, such was the fury (slightly ridiculous at the same time) with which he barked and snapped at my hands and feet, it was all I could do to get away unscathed.

14

Tonight's fireworks didn't help to calm him down. The girls and I had our own particular Grand Firework Display in the back garden—a whole 50p box worth. (The usual trouble with the Catherine wheel jumping off its pin). Tam had to be confined to barracks, otherwise he'd have done himself an injury. We know him well enough by now!

FRIDAY, 15 NOVEMBER

Tam three months with us to the day, and still going strong, touch wood! A fine thank-offering, though, he presents us with this morning.

I was in a bad mood as it was, he'd cried at seven. Fair enough, only neither of the girls would get up (another labour dispute), so in the end I went down myself. There in the middle of the kitchen-mat a great puddle. Tam tries to make up to me, rubbing himself against my leg, then turning over on his back. "You little hypocrite" I thought, "Well, this time I'll give you a taste of your own medicine." So I rubbed his nose in it, the way they say you should. Then I took a scrubbing brush and scrubbed the patch clean. All the while he's standing about on the lino, shame-faced, not knowing where to put himself. Already I felt I'd "over-reacted" (a word they're fond of at the University—apparently, I'm rather prone to it). Then I put him out. He didn't want to go at all—well, it was a frosty morning—and soon cried to be let in again. Then, back into his box he nipped, where he nestled, right in the corner. I went back to bed but couldn't settle.

I spoke to one of the servitors at the University, when I went in to work. He has a big alsation, even though he and his family live in a flat in the centre of Edinburgh. He says he ensures that the dog gets plenty of exercise. Keeps him in trim too. I said to him, "I felt a bit guilty about rubbing his nose in it like that."

"There was no need" he said, "He knows perfectly well he's done wrong. Take our Trixie, the other night she starts crying at half-five, for no apparent reason. I go down, give her a good slap, and back to bed. She's quiet for a few moments, then off she goes again. Usually I let her out at seven. Well, in the end I get up in a filthy mood, dress and grab her for off. She can't wait. Down the stairs, her pulling like mad. Well, hardly is she at the gutter but, whoosh!, like Noah's flood. A good three minutes, I'm not exaggerating. Just think of the agony she must've been in all that time! Then all she did was look up at me, gratefully. What could you do? You're dealing with a creature with feelings just like you and me. Better in some respects. Always remember that."

I suddenly recalled that poor cow left deliberately unmilked, with its udders so full the veins stood out fat, in Ulverston Market years ago, where I was at the Boys' Brigade Camp, and my father saying "You know why it's in that state?—To show it has a good yield. And all for the sake of an extra shilling or two."

15

TUESDAY, 31 DECEMBER

End of first year, so to speak, with "the boy". Marianne says, since we haven't got a son, he's the next best thing to male company. We've got into a reasonable routine with him now, I'm glad to say.

First thing, after he's been out, he gets a handful of dog biscuits (bought loose—they're cheaper that way) in his bowl and a drink of milk in his plastic Summer County Soft Margarine container. That's all he gets till lunchtime at 12 on the dot (Marianne's a stickler for punctuality), when he has some dog-meat ("Bounce" usually, or "Bonus", if they've got a special offer at St Cuthbert's). He has milk with his lunch—never water, he can't stomach it. He always eats his food first, then he has a drink. The milk must never be mixed with the meat and biscuits, otherwise he'll leave the dish alone. Gone are the milk-sap days, he got tired of them after about three weeks— too insipid, I suppose. He eats and drinks with a good appetite, without being greedy. It's good to see him polish off his food, a proper natural function working properly. In the evening he might have a drink, but he doesn't need any food.

1975

WEDNESDAY, 1 JANUARY

Some of our neighbours who've never spoken to us, indeed have looked straight through us when we've greeted them, just as if we were blithering idiots, have started addressing us. But only when we have Tam with us, and usually he's the subject of conversation. Marianne's response—"Well, if that's what they think of us! If we're only of interest if and when we have the dog with us, then they've come to the wrong address. What *you* choose to do is your own decision, but as for me, I'm not letting on. Honestly, some people!"

MONDAY, 13 JANUARY

My 44th birthday. A porridge-bowl full of "Winalot" waiting for me at the breakfast-table, with a doggy card.

"Yes, very witty," I say, "Now bring out the presents." Tam comes in with a Gillette safety-razor-set in his jaws, well, when I say "in his jaws", dragging it and mauling it and wanting a chase. Typical!

THURSDAY, 6 FEBRUARY

Catherine's 11 years old today. She's having a party at this very moment. Well, she's been to so many she has to return the compliment some time. Can't say I like them. I stick here in the front room, staying clear. Tam's with me—restless.

The girls have had their tea, now they're going upstairs. Tam is scratching at the front-room door, crying to be let out into the hall till in the end I give in. He knows very well he's not allowed upstairs.

He's taken up position, standing facing the stairs, listening, raring to go. Oh, all these laughing girls upstairs, how he longs to bounce up and throw himself into that knot of life, to be in the thick of things! All the fun and games he's missing! "How boring it is, waiting here and all that marvellously rich activity just a few yards away, out of my reach." No wonder he's whimpering.

I go back to my books. Suddenly there's a flurry upstairs, and a burst of giggling. I thought as much, he's up there with them. He simply can't resist. I can hear his collar rattling and various squeaks and squeals. The fuss they'll be making of him, all those young girls. His cup of joy is full.

FRIDAY, 7 MARCH

Tam's grown an awful lot lately. He's beginning to thin out nicely, and looks quite lithe, and how long and bushy his tail's become! The older he gets, the more the sheepdog in him comes out.

Take his morning routine. Once he's been out, gobbled his biscuits down, and lapped up his milk, then he's ready for a game. When we're at our lowest ebb, he's most lively—a real Army P.T. Instructor. He can't wait till we're up and doing. "Come on! the birds have already been at it for ages, the sun's up, spring is on the way, and still you lot hardly stir. Can't you see what you're missing?" And swish! he's grabbed something and is flaunting it in front of Catherine for a chase.

SATURDAY, 8 MARCH

Marianne's started working afternoons at a Ladies' Outfitters in Morningside. She works from 1 to 5.30, five days a week. If I haven't got a lecture or class at University, I walk in with her after lunch or fetch her in the late afternoon. I always take Tam with me; he makes sure of that.

I'm sitting reading in the front room by the fire, with Tam snoozing at my feet. At five minutes past five, without my stirring, up he gets, gives himself a shake, and comes and stands at the side of my armchair, jet-black, soundless, looking hard, unblinkingly, with those clear honest eyes of his, intensely alert, ready for off, pleading silently, *willing* me to take him. How can you say no?

It fascinates me, this built-in clock he seems to have inside him. He only needs to do something a few times and a regular habit is established. Of course, we human beings also have a regulator inside us, but we need our clocks and watches. Tam only has his own invisible one, and extremely efficient it is.

TUESDAY, 18 MARCH
St GALL, SWITZERLAND (engaged in a month's research)

Hotel Ekkehard,
Rorschacherstrasse 50

Dear Marianne & girls,
. . . How's the garden?,—coming on O.K.? See you all keep the flowers happy. And what about "the boy", how's he doing? And last, but not least, chiefly yourselves?

Love,
Derek

WEDNESDAY, 26 MARCH

Hotel Ekkehard
Rorschacherstrasse 50

Dear Marianne & girls,
. . . One of the things I did enjoy about going to Kirkby Lonsdale was seeing the daffodils and jonquils on the graves of the churchyard of St Mary's—birth and death, the two mysteries. The tenderness of those tiny jonquils—their flowers almost came up from the ground, they were so small.

Love,
Derek

FRIDAY, 4 APRIL
ZÜRICH

Hotel Krone,
Limmatquai

Dear Marianne & girls,
. . . How are you all? I hope you're all well and thriving in my absence. Don't work too hard now! I wish I could see the garden. A pity you haven't a camera to take a few snaps. I sometimes think about that willow I cut back so drastically in the back garden—I do hope it's recovered. I must learn to be more gentle than my father. It's time I closed, as it's five to midnight.

Lots of love,
Derek

MONDAY, 14 APRIL

What have I come home to? Tam dominates the house, the whole conversation. He's at the gnawing stage, apparently he'll eat anything, but anything.

"As long as he leaves my lobster alone!" I say. It's arrived!—the black 2½ ft long metal sculpture, done by a certain Mr Root of Leicester. Looks splendid, set up there on its stone plinth in the front room. I've paid the £35 it cost in monthly instalments of £5. The carriage, so Marianne tells me, came to all of £22! The men didn't half have a job lugging it in. It may be heavy, but at least it keeps still!

As for "the boy", he's become part and parcel of everything we do. This morning I'm sitting on the bottom stair in the hall, lacing up my shoes, prior to going for a stroll.

"Look out" Marianne shouts from the kitchen, "Here he comes!" She opens the door. Whoosh! Like a black arrow, out he shoots, skids to a halt (if arrows skid), and now he's licking my hands and turning over on his back, now jumping up at me, as I put my coat on.

"Alright, alright. I'll take you". The whole household seems to revolve round him. I'm getting quite jealous.

TUESDAY, 15 APRIL

9.15 am. Back to University. Walking in, it's good exercise. Tam looks out into the hall, sizes up the situation, comes and sits next to my feet, upright, touching me, asking for his walk. Being a good boy. What a shame to have to leave him behind!

WEDNESDAY, 16 APRIL

The girls, still full of Tam, keep telling me about his escapades while I was away. They don't need to. I can see with my own eyes.

"What on earth's that noise?" I said at tea last night, "I can't see any train."

"Oh, that?", answered Elisabeth, "It's only Tam eating the table-leg. You can expect your side to go down any minute now."

"Hope you don't mind", Catherine chips in.

"Oh no, don't mind me."

"Timber!" shout the girls, whereupon "the boy" emerges, chewing.

Beat your termite-colony any day!

But it's no joke. Nowhere's safe from him now. He's forever popping his woolly head into our waste-paper baskets and rummaging about, snatching crumpled paper and worrying it, growling in the process. And matchsticks, they're his staple diet at the moment. The look on his face as he chews one. Blissful isn't in it. There's no drug in them, is there? Like coca or phosphorus. Can you become a phosphorus addict? Must ask Dr B.

Suddenly I remember that phrase from years ago in the classroom, when caught chewing gum. "Empty your mouth in the waste-paper basket!"

THURSDAY, 17 APRIL

He's no better over at the Tennis Club—now the season's started up again. Of course he insists on coming over, our Tam. Has to be in on everything.

The only trouble is, whenever any of the members pick him up and make a fuss of him—which of course they can't help doing, him being what he is—then he wriggles and scratches and bites like a mad thing till he's put down. Even then he won't sit still. No manners!

My goodness! wouldn't he like to be out on court! THAT BALL!

FRIDAY, 18 APRIL

Tam naughty again. Still going through a stage—the "Trotzalter" the Germans call it, "the age of defiance". With children it's usually round about three.

"Of course you do realise, Derek, you're still going through yours?" Marianne tells me.—I'm a late developer, you see.

Be that as it may, Tam's really in the thick of it at the moment. That boy has an appetite for everything, and when I say "appetite", I mean just that.

Occasionally, he's tried lifting the lid of the waste-bin in the kitchen, to snaffle tit-bits. Whenever we catch him at it, we give him what for. He knows very well he shouldn't.

Well, during the night, he'd been at it again. Must've been the fish-smell or something. There's rubbish all over the kitchen floor, kipper-skeletons, tea-leaves, egg-shells, potato-peelings, red wax off the Gouda cheese—the lot. Marianne's just given him a few good slaps with the *Times* (only for top people, note) and such a telling off.

More than any blows it's the rebuke that really gets him. He fairly cowered beneath her words—little thing that he is (though he is growing apace, mind you). Then he whimpered, sorry for himself, if you please, retreated, then finally collapsed backwards into his box, where he's now watching her every move with deep contrition. You should see him.

I mustn't stroke him, otherwise Marianne'll be after me as well.

SATURDAY, 19 APRIL

All he wants (apart from his two good meals a day) is to snatch something, *anything*—a piece of cloth, a slipper, a crumpled-up scrap of paper—dash away with it and be chased. He's no retriever, he doesn't bring things back, he takes them away. Oh, how he loves a chase!

He's tremendously fast, like greased lighting, once released into our back garden. Did I say "our"?—correction, "his". It's his province every bit as much as ours, he's staked out his rights to it.

He'll stand and taunt you. You take up the challenge, pelt after him down to the bottom. Now he's cornered, down by the apple trees. "Got you!" you think. "Oh no, you haven't!" Off he shoots, either through your legs or round you in a flash, and away, asking for more.

How can he be contained? Clearly the real danger's the main road at the front. Marianne's put up a fence (she's the practical one—she does all the dirty work, I do all the talking. "Division of labour" I call it). It's between the side of the house and the wall separating us from our neighbours, so he can't get through there to the front, at least I'd like to think he can't.—Yet. I've seen the way he stands sometimes, looking wistfully through.

He does have a sense of shame though, even guilt, I will say that for him. We soon noticed it—the chink in his armour, if you like. When he's done something he knows is wrong—*and* is found out, that's the point—then he hides his head, drops his now longish tail and lopes off to his box in the kitchen to skulk there, curled up with his black head resting over the side (he's now eaten himself out a little hollow), looking at you with those great eyes of his, mooning. What misery!

You think so? A biscuit, a caress, or a walk in prospect, and in a flash it's forgotten. That resilience of his.

How I do envy him his quick changes of mood!

MONDAY, 21 APRIL

When the girls are due back from school, he gets up from the fire in the front room, shakes himself, rattling his identity disc, goes over to the bay-window and keeps on bobbing up.

—Yes, it's Catherine. The gate's only just banged. (How does he know?)

The trouble is he's still not comfortable with his paws on the window-ledge. Keeps on falling down. But it won't be long before he can scan everything, like so many of the dogs you see round here, appearing at the windows as you walk along the road.

He's growing before our very eyes, lengthening, and his coat's getting fuller, more shaggy. No longer the puppy.

22

TUESDAY, 29 APRIL

I should have told you by now, we also have a guinea-pig called Sam. I assume he's male too, never having gone into the matter closely. Caramel-coloured, 1½ years old, and quite a lad.

Of late Marianne and I have been trying to get dog and guinea-pig used to each other. First stage:

I've taken Sam out of his box (kept in the porch now the weather's warmer) and set him down on the kitchen floor (Tam's territory, you note—well, where isn't downstairs?) The guinea-pig climbs up into Tam's box. The latter intent—up to now the nearest he's got to his mate is sniffing at him through the mesh of his cage—is sitting on his haunches in the middle of the kitchen, watching his every move. Marianne strokes Tam, holding him by his collar, murmuring endearments. Sam bustles about a bit in Tam's box, does a few droppings in a corner, then starts out, to scamper past Tam who nearly snaps at him as he crosses towards the dog's feeding corner by the sink. Aha! has he smelt the dog's milk? Yes. He proceeds to drink, making a funny supping noise and spilling the margarine container in the process, whereupon he drinks up the consequent puddle.

Marianne gingerly lets go of Tam. What will the boy do? Well, first he joins the guinea-pig to polish off the milk, then having sniffed the little fellow, he makes back to his box, roots about the old rug inside, snuffling, then carefully consumes Sam's droppings. Finally he sits inside upright and watches, all alert.

Marianne gathers up Sam and takes him out to put him in his box. I make a fuss of Tam and throw some biscuits into his bowl.

So, you see, a start *has* been made. You don't get lions to lie down with lambs right away. If you must go in for playing on holes of asps, then watch it, my lad!—I've seen enough of them at work to stay clear!

I see, though, those droppings of Sam's will be some inducement. "Every man has his price" (as the cynic said).

THURSDAY, 1 MAY

Is that boy canny? Up to all the tricks, our Tam.

From the start he's been very partial to his toast. Whenever I'm making it at the stove, he's in and out of my legs. Either that, or hanging round me with the love-light in his eyes, watching me put the fresh slices into the bread-basket. To tell you the truth, he prefers it to dog-food, proper meat included.

Now listen to this—I only tumbled to his little game this morning. Really I ought to have realised ages ago.

23

For breakfast, which Marianne and the girls and I take at the table at the window of the living-room (looking out onto the garden), we generally have toast and marge, possibly a boiled egg, marmalade or jam, washed down by tea. During the meal, Tam takes up position under the table, often leaning against my ankles. He loves to lie against you, to touch you.

Breakfast over, Marianne or myself will break the toast (kept German-style in a bread-basket) into fragments, the girls having gone off to school by now. Then one of us will push up the window, generally myself, and toss the bits out onto the "first lawn" for the birds. The birds? Well, as soon as Tam hears the window being pushed up, it's the signal for him to get up and make signs to be let out.

Another pee obviously—and I oblige.

It's odd we hadn't tumbled to his little game before, but I'd be busy clearing the table prior to getting on with the washing up, or Marianne would quite likely have started hoovering the place.

Only this morning, not having anything better to do, after letting the boy out—so insistent he was—I returned to the table and sat and watched. Out he rushes, over the flowers onto the lawn, whereupon he scatters all the birds—no nonsense!—and wolfs down his toast. So that's it, eh? I ought to have known. If the birds are to get anything, he'll have to be kept in.

FRIDAY, 9 MAY

We've taught him not to go upstairs—at least we thought we had. Marianne and I have both been in bed the last couple of days with the 'flu—it's been going the rounds of Edinburgh. The girls say Tam has been utterly at a loss downstairs.

Today he must've heard our voices. We're perking up. Whatever it was, this afternoon, as we both lay there dozing, I heard a scratching on the bedroom door.

"Listen" I said to Marianne, "Can you hear what I hear? I think we've got visitors."

"Come in!" she said.

And in he comes, slowly, unsure of himself. Was he letting himself in for trouble? But he'd been missing us so much he had to risk it. What could you do? I mean, so many of our human rules are purely arbitrary, made simply for our own convenience, aren't they?

You had to laugh.

SATURDAY, 10 MAY

He's growing up so fast it's high time I gave you a snap-shot of him. First he has a lovely coat—firm, strong, jet-black, it fairly gleams with

24

health. You should see him in the sun! The hair's a bit roughish-looking without being wiry, soft to the touch, close-set and rather curly especially about the legs—a trace of spaniel? The tail is now very full, long and bushy. It would almost reach the ground if it didn't curl up like a fox's. The ears are extra-sensitive. Whenever he hears something of vital import, such as "Shall we go for a walk?", or the kettle whistling, or the gate going, then one of those smallish ears of his will immediately go back, close to his head. He has a long sharp nose, the black tip of which is always cold, wet and glistening, a sign of health, I believe.

But I hasten to assure you the dog doesn't entirely monopolize our attention. The great world outside also makes its claims. No, the big venture at the moment is a second-hand car for Germany this summer. I've been to a few places after one. It's like entering a new world—"the trade", they call it.

In a yard along Morningside, this young salesman, grinning all over his face, climbs into a mini ("one careful owner"), and switches on the engine. Engine won't start. He leans out—cigar and half a yard of cuff.

"No petrol. Obvious." he says from the window below us, then gets out, and pushes the mini out of the yard without turning a hair.

Then the RAC man, who's conducted a test on another car we're after, rings us and offers to sell us his own instead.

"A bargain at £500. Rust? Doesn't mean a thing.
You're talking to an expert. I *know* my cars."

SATURDAY, 17 MAY

We've taken the plunge, and got our car. Bought it yesterday. An Austin 1100, 1973 vintage, harvest gold. £720, and two years to pay. Marvellous! Hardly is it displayed in all its splendour in our front garden but Tam, with his usual sense of the occasion, walks out, sniffs it, then thoughtfully christens it. Well, since we didn't have any champagne.

SATURDAY, 24 MAY

Loves his car, does our Tam. He knows exactly what the word means. You say "Are you coming in the car?" and my goodness me! that tail of his doesn't half start wagging. Like a shaggy windscreen-wiper. A wonder he doesn't wear it out! And if the car door happens to be open while Marianne's cleaning out the inside, then in he jumps, climbs onto the back seat and sits there, looking out, large as life. You knock, and he barks back. Great fun!

SUNDAY, 25 MAY

He used to cry to be let out at seven; now he's quiet, he knows someone's coming. When Marianne's let him out and he's had his biscuits, and I still have to come downstairs, he takes up position, curling up "cirque couchant", leaning against the bottom stair. Loyal, expectant. The carpet where he lies is warm to the touch. What a tonic to find such a cordial welcome at that hour of the day! What would we do without him?

SATURDAY, 31 MAY

Whenever one of us, especially the girls, is doing anything to the car, then he likes to be in on it. Same when I'm digging in the back or pottering about the place, watering the house-plants. *Any* activity in fact. He's especially pleased when a number of people are engaged in work or play. I wonder if he can tell the two apart, or is it only we human beings who make the distinction?

How he enjoys it when we wash the car!—all that soapy water being splashed about, all that splendid activity as we rub the glistening "corn-gold" surface to and fro with our shammies, especially when the girls are busy with me, and the sun's shining off the car, and we're all larking about. He's so excited by it all, barking and jumping. In his element. Yes, like Pip's Joe Gargery, he loves a lark.

MONDAY, 2 JUNE

I'm sitting in our front room at my table. I have these four M.A. dissertations to assess for Friday as external examiner for Newcastle University. The sun's streaming into the bay-window which faces due south. I can't concentrate on my work, I'm so engrossed in Tam— the way he's irresistibly drawn to the brightest patch of sunlight on the fitted green carpet. There he rests, his coal-black coat glistening, luxuriating and yet alert. Not asleep. Oh no! Sunlight needs you, you don't just laze in it. You let it soak into you, the sheer goodness of it.

Then, as the sun moves across the sky, shifting the bright patches across the carpet, from time to time he'll get up and slowly assume his new sunlit position. Of late he's come to vary his lying positions. Now, for instance, he's not lying there rounded like a cat; no, he's in what I call a "sphinx posture", flat out, his paws out-stretched before him (just as they are when he's on the alert in a ball game, the object being guarded between them). And all the time taking in the warm blessing of sunlight.

26

He's spot-lighted. Unconsciously, as with all the best art, he makes himself the *centre* of attraction. He's all one, I am somehow splayed. He concentrates on the here and now; I'm torn between past and future, there's always some worry at the back of my mind. That direct animal life of his, his sharp appetite for experience.

I sigh and return to my marking.

TUESDAY, 4 JUNE

Of course he can be a bit of a trial sometimes, Tam, but I'll say this for him, unlike human beings, he never goes in for *wanton* destruction, hooliganism. There's always a purpose to what he does.

Take his treatment of my beloved flower-beds. He simply walks over them, whenever he feels like it on his way from A to B. Not trampling, simply walking. He makes no distinction between flower-beds and lawns, just as he doesn't distinguish plants from weeds. He doesn't root in the soil, he doesn't scrabble at bushes or scratch up flowers, nor have I ever seen him bury a bone in the garden. But it's *his* territory, the garden—let's be quite clear about that—every bit as much as mine. He may be reasonably domesticated, but he's no captive, oh no! He has his rights; he can assert himself, if need be—which is all to the good.

SATURDAY, 21 JUNE

What he loves most of all, endearments aside, is a good game. He'll take something, anything he can get his teeth into, and, with it in his mouth, come towards you at the ready, looking up at you, taunting you, springy, after a chase. You snatch at the object. Right! he recoils. Then, if pursued into the house, he dashes off to hide under the living-room table, arm-chairs or under our low sideboard. Strangely, he'll make no effort to get away; he feels completely safe there.

It's his refuge, our rickety sideboard, the right-hand side, by the door. What a job he has scrambling under, now he's got bigger! First he has to stretch out, bending his long back, finally pulling himself in to safety—a real scramble without any of his usual dignity.

And there he'll lie, naughty, panting, those dark eyes wide, at the ready, with his booty between his forepaws. Down under, safe—or so he seems to think, in spite of being hauled out times without number to be chastised. Or is he just playing along? I saw this film about dolphins the other day on television. I wonder if dogs, like dolphins, aren't a good deal more sophisticated than we think—like children and primitives, so-called?

27

SUNDAY, 22 JUNE

You see it manifesting itself again and again, that need of his to snatch things and be chased by us. Here's the pattern when any of us come home or come down in the morning. Take my return from church today.

Hardly does he see me enter the hall, but he rushes ahead of me into our little cloakroom. Usually there's something or other resting on top of the orange-boxes in which the shoes are kept (the guinea-pig is also housed in the cloakroom over the winter, as it's quite cosy in there)—perhaps a glove, a ski-cap or a scarf. Or he may pinch a slipper, shoe or sandal. Then, with the object clenched between his teeth, he bounces about you, flaunting it in front of you, demanding a chase. Even after being slapped time and time again with a slipper or a rolled-up newspaper (you're not supposed to use your bare hands) for his thieving ways, when it comes to the pinch, he simply cannot resist the urge. It's like a spring constantly surging up in him.

How he loves a ball—*any* ball! It's virtually impossible to take him across playing-fields if there's a football-match in progress. Even on a lead he's like a mad thing, barking and leaping the whole time. He watches the football on television avidly, following every move, rivetted. Indeed his favourite programme is "Match of the Day", followed by "The World About Us", which he watches for the animals. This shows he's got taste.

The other week I bought him a little hard, bright blue ball from William Kay's, along Morningside Road, one of those high bouncers (a larger "super-ball" in fact). He takes it everywhere with him, keeps it in his box, even has it near to him when he's feeding. This afternoon I've been watching him dribble with it down the garden, knocking it from paw to paw, barking away. He got a shock though, when he went crash! into the rose-bush. That took the wind out of his sails for a minute or two. He came back and lay down next to Marianne in her deck-chair on the "second lawn". (I notice, however, he brought the ball with him).

He likes to maul it, bite it so hard the saliva fairly froths over it. If I take it, or rather wrest it from his jaws, with him straining and growling, finally to throw it down the garden for him, my hands are all sticky.

Indoors, he sends it whizzing about, bouncing off the furniture, off the skirting-boards or radiators, just as a large ball-bearing will shoot from spring to spring in a pin-ball machine. It's a frequent noise these days about the house, the thud of the ball, followed shortly by the dry scratch of Tam's claws as he slides bodily across the slippy nigger-brown floorboards around the beige carpet of our living-room. Then, once he has that live little beast of a ball safely lodged in his jaws, again he comes towards you, tingling with alertness, brown eyes wide with life, with affection, excitement, love of the game.

28

You don't let on. "All right then!" he seems to say, "I'll make it easier for you." He drops the ball, traps it with one of his paws, pushes it a little towards you, looking up at you from his sphinx posture sharply, slyly, good-naturedly, to see what you'll do now— "Come on then, come on! Let's be having you! How can I get Master going?"

Then if you still don't let on, he'll prod the ball forward with his nose, nearer and nearer, intensely aware of you and any pounce you might make, glancing up at you, then down at the ball. I think of Stanley Mathews in his heyday, and of my time as a schoolmaster and those teenage upstarts I had to deal with. This universal propensity of drawing opponents on, daring them, the young Turks (of whatever colour) against the Old Guard, revolution threatening the establishment. Young versus old, a natural process.

You dart at the ball. Snap! it's back between his teeth, safe. Off he springs to right or left. "Got you there, eh!" Or suddenly he backs away, tremendously fast, always.

WEDNESDAY, 2 JULY

Marianne's been working part-time at a fashion shop in Morningside. She's been there over three months now, quite likes it too.

She got this afternoon off, and relaxed in a deck-chair in the warmth of our front porch. Tam lay at her feet in a patch of sunlight, leaning against the front-doorstep. She was reading her "Woman". (I remember my mother used to say of such magazines, "I do like a good book", and when I started taking "The Listener" as a schoolboy at the Liverpool Institute, she'd remark "An awful lot of reading there, Derek").

Tam snoozed comfortably, just the odd sigh. No trace of the anxiety that so racked him when he first entered our home.

SATURDAY, 5 JULY

This morning I drove out to the Borders to take the boy to the kennels. (Gwyneth, a school friend of Catherine's, recommended the lady).

For a couple of days Tam has sensed there's something in the offing, and that something is unpleasant. I remember the cat I had as a boy, how it knew when we were going away on holiday, and wandered round the house like a lost soul, rubbing itself against my legs.

The kennels are attached to a bungalow. I go round the back with Tam. The sound of dogs, baying, yapping, howling everywhere. The woman must really love dogs to put up with that the whole time!

We have to take out an insurance policy for him, there in the woman's kitchen (with Tam whimpering beside me)! The premium is 41p. To think we'd claim the £2 we paid for him! She must get some tough customers.

FRIDAY, 15 AUGUST

Today's the first anniversary of Tam's arrival. I write this, bumping along in the hovercraft from Calais to Dover on our way home. Fancy remembering such a date, when I can't even get my daughters' birthdays straight!

TUESDAY, 19 AUGUST

This morning I drove over with Marianne and the girls to fetch Tam from the kennels. Tam terribly subdued, not himself at all. The girl said, yes, he'd had his walk every day, she'd taken him herself.

It must have been the hours and hours of being penned in a cage that got him down. What's more, he'd been on his own. He looks dreadfully thin. I feel quite guilty. Marianne said

"We'll think twice about putting him in again".

"I agree".

But what can you do, if you want to get away?

THURSDAY, 21 AUGUST

Tam perking up at last. I reckon it's the whistle of the kettle that's done the trick. As soon as it goes, his tail starts to wag. He'd been missing his tea. That's what it was.

FRIDAY, 22 AUGUST

Went for a walk in the evening with Catherine and Tam. The boy is still rather timid outdoors. Jibbed at the footbridge over the Braid Burn, down Hermitage Dell. I think it was the gaps between the planks that unsettled him.

SATURDAY, 23 AUGUST

Took Tam in with me to fetch my mail from the University. Walked up the stairs to the tenth floor. Good exercise. Tam reluctant, very uneasy on them—they're plastic covered; he kept on slithering. He doesn't seem to like the idea of skyscrapers either. Well, he's not the only one. It's the same with the top-deck of the 41 bus.

SUNDAY, 24 AUGUST

A big step forward for "the boy", or shall I call him "young buck"? I've just witnessed him performing his initiation rite on our top lawn.

Instead of standing with legs slightly astraddle, behold! he tentatively lifts a leg, not against anything, but into the air—a wonder he kept his balance—and dribbles his water out to the side. Deadly serious he is about it, at the same time slightly puzzled.

A whole new world is opening up for him.

MONDAY, 25 AUGUST

It's not just cupboard love with him, he'll forego a meal to accompany the girls. He just doesn't like being on his own.

How he loves a walk! As soon as he senses I'm about to fetch Marianne from the shop, first he goes and patiently watches me put my shoes on, then stands under his lead which hangs in the hall by the back door. If that's not a hint, what is?

And doesn't he race along Cluny Gardens if given half a chance! (on the lead of course). The sheep-dog in him. To look at him, the best part's border-collie, but there's also a dash of spaniel, seen in his rather woolly fetlocks and the curly tail, and possibly a pinch of labrador in his gentle nature. Certainly a rare, nay, unique mixture. Bags of life! Perfectly fitted to his purpose, true, affectionate, sound. Of course he doesn't belong to us. He's entrusted to us.

"You naughty boy! you must *not* eat that blanket!" shouts Elisabeth from the kitchen. He's at it again.

"Get out of there!" A good-natured growl. "Oh, look at the mess he's made!"

—In all a splendid fellow.

SUNDAY, 31 AUGUST

Tam off his food. It must be the heat; usually he's no trouble.

As regards his feeding habits, he's still crazy on toast. The noise he makes when he crunches it! Apart from his early morning biscuits, he used to have two big meals a day, mid-day and evening, but now he's older, he only has one proper meal, at 12 noon. Marianne generally prepares it. It consists of ⅓ of a tin of "Bounce" with some "Winalot" biscuits crumbled in it, and milk to drink in his container. He still insists on food and drink being separate.

We keep the fork we use to get out the "Bounce" scrupulously apart from our own cutlery. Nor is the dog ever allowed to use any of our crockery. We never throw him scraps from the table, though we do sometimes put some of our leftovers into his bowl. He never gets fried food.

His feeding-place is under the hatch between our kitchen and the living-room, near the sink. We keep a newspaper under his bowl and drinking container, so he doesn't leave a mess, but there's no need really; he's not a messy dog. He never drags food about the floor now. Woe betide you, though, if you disturb him while feeding! It's more than your life's worth.

WEDNESDAY, 3 SEPTEMBER

Boiling hot day. Tam panting after any exertion, his mouth wide open, his long pink tongue hanging out.

SATURDAY, 6 SEPTEMBER

Out gardening with Tam. I've always liked my flowers, Tam too—so much so, that he's not averse to eating the occasional flower-head, probably out of curiosity, as much as anything. I'm glad to say, however, he doesn't seem to have made a habit of it.

With his customary sensitivity to our feelings, I believe he shares our love for the garden and everything in it. Mind you, he does tend to treat my "found sculpture" as I call it, an odd-shaped cluster of roseroots, about a foot square, a little roughly, knocking it about the lawns, worrying it, butting it and growling in the process.

Funny to see him snatch one of the long canes as I kneel and stake the chrysanthemums, then try to dash off with it. What a job he has! as the end of it scrapes the ground, acting as a brake, wheeling him round. I only hope he doesn't tear his mouth.

Like any robin, he enjoys seeing me dig or plant, any work in fact, and will, after a spot of exercise, station himself nearby, lying doggo, watching me. The montbretia clumps are favourite cushions, he hasn't half flattened them! But he hates me to make a fire in the incinerator, barking at the flames as if they were live things. The same with the lawn-mower. He's chary too if ever I smoke my pipe; a match lit anywhere near causes him to flinch.

It started raining late in the afternoon, while I was working out at the back, and I took shelter in the shed down at the bottom by the apple trees. Hardly had I sat down on the old battered mat by the open shed door, but he came and joined me (he doesn't like rain either), lying against me, supine, drowsy. I lifted him onto my lap and stroked him, my hands all dry against his coat. You could feel the glad warmth radiating from him.

SUNDAY, 7 SEPTEMBER

Another warm day with plenty of insect-life about. I've noticed that blue-bottles, bees and wasps all fascinate Tam. This afternoon I watched him handle a fly. He'd become aware of it buzzing and crawling up the window of the livingroom.

There he sits, upright as always, as straight-backed as Goethe in his old age, intently watching every move the fly makes. He's as still as a snake, only his eyes moving. Then with a pounce, he brings the insect down. There it is, buzzing about the floor. He assumes his sheep-dog posture before it, body stretched out flat, fore-paws extended, ready for a game.

Whenever the creature tries to crawl off, or to dart to right or left, he immediately blocks it. His paws are now pads, the claws sheathed so as not to wound. He then contemplates the fly's antics with a scientific keenness, not to say delight, for he seems to radiate enjoyment. Not that he torments it, as a cat will a mouse. No, he merely keeps it under control, watching to see what it will do next. This isn't always easy for him, the fly is quick and he can hardly grip such an insubstantial creature. He has to bring down the pads of his paws smartish but without flattening the fly. Remarkable, how delicately he does this. Finally he tires and pops it into his mouth, seemingly to eat it. Aha! he feels a buzzing and a whirring within. He opens his mouth and out pops the victim and away. He stares open-mouthed.

Other times he'll try to swallow such small prey down as fast as possible. But generally he'll first give any insect a run for its money.

WEDNESDAY, 17 SEPTEMBER

"The boy's" not well, not well at all. He's lying there under the sideboard, thoroughly sorry for himself, afflicted with a hacking cough like a child with croup. Dull, floppy, as if he were about to die any minute. If he gets up, it's to stand a foot away from the wall, facing it for ages. We're all down.

This afternoon Elisabeth and Catherine went to the People's Dispensary for Sick Animals along George IV Bridge to get Tam a tonic. ("Put him on a bottle" as my grannie used to say). Now they're back with some smallish white tablets, which we've crushed and slipped into a little milk. He's just drunk the potion. Let's hope he'll benefit, but to tell you the truth, I have my doubts regarding those tablets. They look just like the ones they gave us for Jock, our budgerigar (now sadly defunct), when he had his cyst. What a business that operation was in the dispensary! I must say, though, that coloured doctor conducted it beautifully. The lump was on the bird's back. The surgeon made me hold Jock, showing me the exact way to clasp his breast. Then he took a piece of cotton, tied it round the lump and tugged it tight till it made a small bulb (like the "cherries" I'd make as a boy with bits of burst balloon), then, with his scalpel, carefully opened up the cyst and scraped out the yellow granulated contents, like the inside of a fig, wiped it clean, and applied ointment. The poor wee mite almost passed away under my hands, Catherine watching the whole time. Later she sat with the bird in her clasped hands, perfectly still, as I drove home carefully, so he wasn't jogged. He recovered, and had a few more months.

—So let's not despair. There's life in the young dog yet.

FRIDAY, 19 SEPTEMBER

Tam picking up. He's found his appetite again. Stole a slipper today, which is always a good sign.

TUESDAY, 23 SEPTEMBER

Back to normal. Elisabeth's resumed her "modern tap" lessons along St Stephen's Street. A great dancer, our Liz. Tam "gets hep" (as they used to say) whenever she tries out any of her steps in the front room. Has he the talent to be a proverbial "dancing dog"?

FRIDAY, 26 SEPTEMBER

I've got awful tooth-trouble. Sometimes I think they're more bother than they're worth. Tam busy dropping his own teeth all over the house. In sympathy? Apparently he simply eats them up—or so the girls tell me.

This morning I opened his jaws to see if there were any gaps. Hardly a protest from him. Goodness! how fierce he looks when his mouth is drawn back, exposing those leathery purplish gums of his! What beautiful teeth he has, though—fine, white, sharp and sound. I only wish I had a set like his.

SATURDAY, 28 SEPTEMBER

If ever the girls and I start dancing and prancing about in the front room to the gramophone, then Tam's sure to come rushing in to join us, and immediately he'll be scampering in and out of our legs, barking like mad, cavorting in his own way, then suddenly keeling over to lie flat on his back and have his tummy tickled. Once that's done, off he'll shoot to snatch something, wanting to be chased. Always the same.

But if there's a fight on television, like tonight's film, a western, with men throwing each other all over the show, he gets all upset. He'll approach the screen, stand a foot away, facing it and, obviously distressed, bark at the goings-on. Strangely, "grand" scenes of war with artillery firing or bombs exploding, don't disturb him as much as people fighting hand to hand. The truth of the matter is he prefers concord to discord at home. He's like the Psalmist:

"Behold how good and how pleasant it is for brethren to dwell together in unity! It is like the precious ointment upon the head that ran down upon the beard, even Aaron's beard."

It's no exaggeration to say discord alarms him. If I lose my temper and start banging about the place, or any of us raise our voices to each other, then poor Tam doesn't known which way to turn. Do you know?, Marianne and I can even upset him by pretending to have a row. Then he'll seek the refuge of his lair, either his box in the kitchen, or, more likely, under the sideboard, and there he'll skulk, keeping out of harm's way. But as soon as he senses I'm in a good mood again (doesn't take long), then out he comes from under the sideboard, flattening his back in the process, to make friends with me. His tail wagging vigorously, he's so glad the storm's over.

It would be crude to describe his attitude as wheedling. No, I'd unsettled him by my roughness, and now he needed to reassure himself of my renewed goodwill. He shares our feelings fully, painfully even.

You can learn from that boy!

WEDNESDAY, 1 OCTOBER

Today late afternoon I went for a stroll with Tam round Morningside. Ferocious encounter with a cat.

We're walking along opposite the entrance to the Andrew Duncan Clinic when Tam suddenly stiffens at a gateway. There, on top of the privet hedge sits this horrible fat old cat. Tam jumps up instinctively, whereupon it hisses viciously, its eyes ablaze, and stabs at Tam. Fortunately the stab missed, otherwise he'd have lost an eye.

Whenever he sees, hears or smells a cat in a garden during our walks, you can feel his every fibre ready for battle. If ever there's one in our back garden, he claws at the back door, desperate to be released. You open up and away he pelts, barking furiously. I bet he can beat any greyhound or whippet, he's so lean and fit. In the pink.

SATURDAY, 4 OCTOBER

He has a thing about doors. Well, they *are* important, aren't they? (I've had a number closed on me in my time!) He can open certain ones by standing up on his hind-legs and pressing on them—he soon learned that—while for others he needs our assistance. As a rule, when he wants to leave a room and the door's shut, then he'll just station himself by it, sitting there silently, waiting for you to get up and open it for him. If it's an urgent matter, he may cry, but it's a dignified appeal; he doesn't whine or snivel. Again that inherent dignity of his—I maintain he's a prince of the blood or, at the very least, one of Nature's gentlemen.

Once I open a door, he'll delay for a moment, looking up at me. I've sometimes wondered, is there some primitive fear in him of being jammed? Once he's looked up and been reassured that the way is clear, out he trots.

What impels him to leave a room?—All sorts of things. He's especially fond of children, from toddlers to teenagers, and loves to be right in amongst them. Catherine's busy playing "elastics" in the back with a couple of the neighbour's children. Poor thing! he's crying at the back door this very moment. How he'd love to be right in amongst them! The only trouble is he'd spoil their game.

His idea of bliss is to be rushing around in amongst a cluster of children at play, a whole heap of them laughing, jumping, tossing things about, running here, there and everywhere from one to the other, in the thick of it, then, when at last things quieten down, to settle, nestle close, be petted.

All good clean fun. Fun—that's what draws him. St Augustine's "dilectio", delight, "the force that makes the life-time strong", the urge that shapes the course our lives take, for we are creatures just like him, with appetites just like his.

THURSDAY, 9 OCTOBER

This morning about 9.45 am driving to work, stuck in a queue of cars along Mayfield Road, I saw a man walking a dog like Tam—border collie, only with a lot more white than black to his coat. A "doggy dog" (as Robert Garioch, the poet, once called our Tam). The dog was trotting along close to the walls of the tiny gardens the houses have there (a couple of feet, that's all there is between them and the façades), and proceeding in a docile fashion, without a lead (something we'd never dream of allowing Tam to do).

Do you know?, when the dog reaches a certain house, a big fluffy English sheep-dog suddenly pops up at the window, barks and drops down, obviously eager to be let out. Now how did it know? Telepathy, hearing, smell, that built-in clock? Were the man and his dog in the habit of walking along there at that time every day?

—But to appear at that very instant?

I do know this. Our Tam has the keenest of senses. How sensitive those ears of his are! When he sits in the garden after consuming his toast, taking in the scene, watching the birds flit about, those thin ears of his seem constantly to be registering data as they prick up or jerk back, often singly. Whenever we're talking, and there's some message of special import for him, then it's this quick jerking back of the ears that indicates most clearly his attentiveness.

FRIDAY, 10 OCTOBER

He's on a different wave-length from me. He can tell when Catherine's coming along Cluny Gardens on her way back from school at 3.45, even before our iron gate grates. And when he rushes to the bay-window, his tail wagging vigorously, his movements are equally delicate, sensitive. He hardly grazes, far less scrapes or jars my metal lobster-sculpture which stands in the way, nor does he ever knock over any of the flower-pots on the low table by the window.

By contrast, Sam, our guinea pig, an eighth of his size, can cause havoc if let loose in the front room. Mind you, he has different interests. "He's after his greens" the girls say, so he has no qualms whatsoever about perching up on his little hind-legs in order to wrench at the protruding leaves of the house plants. How ridiculous he looks!—those little legs and pink feet and the fat bottom—but he's a menace, make no mistake. Cacti, wandering sailor, ivy, begonia, even my pineapple plant—they're all one to him, just so long as they're green and edible. Standing up, he tugs at the nearest (I don't believe his eyesight's very good), wrenches off a piece, falls to munching it, then he stands up again, tugs at another so hard it tumbles down. Soon there's soil and upset plants all over the carpet.

Sam blunders about amongst things (though I will say this for him, he can fairly scamper for cover). He'll knock over his feeding bowl and waterbowl, and Tam's plastic container too, unlike Tam who I've never seen upset any of them. Nor would Tam ever snatch Sam's lettuce off him, while the latter stands there, "safe" under the arm-chair in the living-room munching it, his chubby caramel-coloured jaws working away.

The truth is Sam's *piggish*.

What a silly old porky face he has, for such a little creature, with his prominent rodent teeth, his fat cheeks and no neck! Looking at him, I'm reminded of Trudie, the androgynous tortoise we owned when we lived in St Albans. That ancient primaeval face of Trudie's and the way he used to love his lettuce. Another one crazy on "greens". That small bulgy rough purplish tortoise tongue, creased down the middle like a parrot's. I can see Marianne there in our garden along Camp Road, in the sun, feeding Trudie his lettuce and stroking his scaly head as he feeds quietly, then he makes off to root about in the rich pile of compost and mulch down by the fence, just as Sam curls up right inside his cage of sweet meadow-hay.

No, Tam for all his animality, has more dignity. He's at a higher level than Sam. He takes more care, is able to be more considerate, knows more sympathy.

SATURDAY, 11 OCTOBER

Tam needs to make his presence felt. And why not?, since it's a good one.

He's very fond of our postman and jumps up at him whenever we have to open the door, like today, when I went down in my pyjamas at 7.45. I've a suspicion the postman enjoys knocking us up when he thinks we're having a lie-in. But he likes Tam too and makes a fuss of him.

Yes, anyone, anything that impinges on us from the outside world, immediately stirs the boy. "Irritability"—that's what the teacher used to call it in my "General Science" lessons at school years ago. I never had a proper scientific training (as you may have guessed). At the time, I remember thinking it a poor way of expressing one of the signs of a living organism. It reminded me of my father's "crankiness" (as we children called it), his rattiness, occasional abruptness, when he came home from work at the British American Tobacco Company in Liverpool. I don't think he was fulfilled in his job.

This gift or quality of Tam's, however, is a wonderfully sensitive alertness, affectionate as well as wary. Tam *appreciates* the here and now. Human beings, I'm afraid, can't endure for long the demands of such an attitude, and so they dull it almost systematically, they harden and callous themselves. There are a variety of drugs available for the purpose. But what a shame, to lessen this availability, this openness to experience!

WEDNESDAY, 15 OCTOBER

I'm walking in to work nowadays. This morning, as I sat on the bottom stair, putting on my shoes, who should join me, but your friend and mine. Nothing quite like a WALK.

Anticipating this great treat, he's giving himself a good shake, rattling his collar and chinking his disc. He's also developed the habit of stretching. First he'll extend his front legs right out, then stretch his long back—how whippy that young spine!—then out go his back legs in an ecstacy of expectation, luxurious yet purposeful, getting himself in trim.

—Such a pity to have to disappoint him, but one can't conduct tutorials with a dog in attendance.

MONDAY, 20 OCTOBER

"Give me your paw" you say, and he does, oh, so readily! time and time again, even when you're long fed up. I push him away, and back comes that paw. The insatiable need he has for reassurance, part of his sensitivity, and loyalty.

Where does it come from, this bond? "We love Him because He first loved us".

SATURDAY, 25 OCTOBER

This morning the girls and I went into town on the 41 bus, a splendid great Leyland Atlantean. We go upstairs of course, Tam scuttling up rather unwillingly. We sit down, and Tam immediately lies down, flat out, under our seat, again clearly ill at ease on this moving vehicle. I don't think he likes the surface of the floor either; whenever we go round corners he winces and cowers. He hates being off balance—I think that's what it is primarily. It's the disorientation that scares him, and the sense that he can do nothing about it.

He's not a timid creature at all in normal circumstances. This afternoon, when Catherine and I took him along Blackford Glen Road, by Craigmillar Park Golf Course, he wasn't at all afraid of the horses and ponies in the field there. On the contrary, he stood up on his hind legs, placed his paws on the wall—he's fully grown now—and merely looked inquisitively at their faces. Rather pleased with them by all accounts, if his tail was anything to go by. He didn't bark at these calm fellow creatures, even when they snorted, flicking away the odd fly crawling about the corners of their large brown eyes. As I say, he's not the yapping or yelping kind, our Tam.

FRIDAY, 7 NOVEMBER

Rainy day, no lectures, I spend my time at home reading. Tam is at my feet by the fire, in fact he's lying against it virtually. The gas-fire in the front room stands on brass legs about 4 inches high. Tam, in order to get the full benefit of its heat, has taken up his sphinx posture with his front paws extended under it. He holds his smallish sleepy head so close to its red bars that I can't help wondering how he doesn't singe himself. How can he possibly stand so much heat?

Now he's changed his position, he's lying flopped out on his side, showing all he's got, with his back to the fire. Now, having absorbed all the heat he can take, he lopes away, dopey, to slide under our Ercol couch by the far wall, there to lie, outstretched, cooling off. Again he exposes his belly, which is slightly pink, as opposed to the blackness of his coat. No shame.

Rainy days make him lethargic (as it can children—ask any infant teacher). You can hardly believe he could be so floppy, after seeing him so sprightly. But just let the sun come out and in a flash he's transformed.

THURSDAY, 13 NOVEMBER

During the nine o'clock news Tam suddenly got all restless. We let him out, whereupon we heard a scuffling and a loud barking from him in the back garden. I went out with Marianne, armed with a torch, to see what was the matter.

Lo and behold! a hedgehog, standing there in amongst the fuchsias, and Tam intent, not striking but ready to pounce (perhaps he's been pricked already). The hedgehog doesn't stir in the light of our torch. He seems alert and yet utterly remote from us. Marianne and I rush in to fetch the girls, but by the time we come out it's gone and all our searching is to no avail.

I remember that hedgehog Marianne pointed out to me early one morning years ago, crossing the lawn of Miss Robinson's house in Bassett, Southampton, where we lodged in the early days of our marriage. I've seen so many hedgehogs flattened on roads. And those toads—we counted 70 at least—flattened one Easter on the road by Pitlochry, caught crossing over to spawn in a pond.

"Keep your eyes skinned, Derek", my father always used to say when we went out walking into the country from Norris Green, Liverpool, where I spent my boyhood.

SATURDAY, 15 NOVEMBER

Whenever we all have to go out, leaving Tam on his own, he looks very sad. Until recently, we made him get in his box, kept in the kitchen by the gas-boiler. Latterly, however, he's insisted on being given a freer run of the house.

Once he realises we're going out and he can't come, then he smartly plants himself under the chair in the hall, under the couch in the front room (if the door happens to be open), or under the sideboard—always *under* something, something preferably low—and he'll lie flat on his belly, watchful, snapping at whoever tries to get him out. This is one of the very few occasions when he growls or snaps. Psychologists speak of "sensory deprivation". I suppose that's what he feels is in store for him, pent up in our kitchen, so he's ensuring he finds somewhere which allows him to roam at large. He's come to assert himself more, to insist on certain rights. But he has a point; you can trust him, he's well out of the gnawing stage.

The same at bed-time, now that he's got tired of always sleeping in his box—how battered it's become from his depredations!—he's started demanding other places to sleep. So once he sees us switching off lamps and fires and filling our hot water-bottles, he takes up position in one of his lairs. Nowadays he often sleeps overnight at the foot of the stairs.

How glad he is, though, when at last we're back from an outing, or when we come down in the morning! He can leap up to my chin, in welcome. Instinctively I push him away for fear he'll mark my clothes, but really I don't need to, for he almost invariably keeps himself scrupulously clean. Often you see him, sitting in front of the fire, licking himself. Occasionally he may smell of sweat when he's been out running, especially in muggy weather. It's a slightly rank, tarry smell, rather like creosote, acrid but not unpleasant. Not like "Lady the brach" in "King Lear" who "sits by the fire and stinks".

SATURDAY, 22 NOVEMBER

Tam, frightened of the washing-machine, skulking in the hall. Well, it does kick up a bit of a racket. Later however, when Marianne hangs out the washing in the back garden, he'll have to be in on it. All those flapping sheets and garments. Great fun!

He's not a timid dog, but he *is* chary of machines, whether buses or washing-machines, and I've noticed he gives car exhausts a wide berth, but he's not afraid of any creature, dog or man.

Nor would I call him highly strung, as thoroughbreds so often are. No, he has all the steadiness of your confirmed mongrel. I can't help thinking Mother Nature likes the bloods to be mixed. Like Tam himself, she likes a bit of sport, a spot of experimentation.

That doesn't mean, of course, that he's not sensitive, acutely so, with an intelligence that matches that of many an academic I've known, if by intelligence you mean the gift of sizing up a situation and doing what has to be done.

Those eyes of his, so rightly called the "windows of the soul", now brown, now steely grey—the colour seems to vary according to the light—how vivid they are, how piercing! The world seems to go straight into them.

SUNDAY, 23 NOVEMBER

A further progress report on the relationship betwen Sam and Tam: We've had to wait till Tam grew up before attempting to influence their attitude to one another. As a puppy, he was just too unpredictable. As might be expected, he was jealous of any attention given to Sam, especially stroking. At first we wondered, was it safe to have them out together? Would Tam instinctively chase after this little scampering creature, strike him down and wound him? There's no feline cruelty in Tam, but there's no doubt about it, he can be ferocious on occasions. Even playfully, he might do the little fellow a mischief.

It was mainly Marianne who conducted the operation. She's good at such things. Besides, as she predicted, she's been the one who's fed and looked after the pets, thereby gaining their confidence. She always made sure that if she held Sam, she simultaneously patted Tam on his smallish black head, murmuring endearments. The guinea-pig would give a high-pitched chunner, while Tam kept an earnest silence.

The acid test came earlier this evening, when, in full view of Tam, Marianne put out a carrot for Sam in the middle of the floor of our living-room. What would Tam do? Would he snatch it away and gobble it up? No, not as long as he got one himself from Marianne, although it's by no means a favourite delicacy of his.

You should see them now, gnawing and crunching their carrots, the dog watchfully, the guinea-pig nervily (he always has to snatch his carrot to safety under an armchair). Tam's jaws move loud and long, Sam's short and fast. Lean, black dog, podgy, caramel and white guinea-pig, both at home, getting on all right with each other.

Sam, having consumed his fill, nips into a favourite corner by our standard-lamp and does a dribble onto the dark brown floor-boards, producing a clear pool about the size of two old pennies, to be shortly followed by four or five little, hardish, khaki-coloured pellets, of the size and shape of liquorice torpedoes, which, when broken open, are of a bright yellow hue. Tam glances across, interested, then once the little fellow's finished (he'd never interrupt him on the job), he goes over, sniffs, then eats up the droppings with obvious relish—more, I reckon, than he's shown while eating his carrot. You should see him licking his chops.

So here we have a beautiful example of a "closed ecological system" (to use the current jargon). I'm convinced this provision of "goodies" by Sam has helped to cement the friendship between the two animals. One good turn deserves another.

FRIDAY, 28 NOVEMBER

You should see him at night, when he's been rooting about, roaming on his own out there in the garden, and I open our back door, sending out a shaft of light, and call out "Tam, Tam! Come in, Tam." I can see the shadowy figure looking my way, but no response. He's decided to stay out a bit longer, he's asserting his will a little, that spirit I so much admire both in human beings and animals—mettle, individuality, holding on to personal freedom at all costs.

But then a little later I open the door, call out "Tam, come and get your tea." He can't hold out any longer (whatever it is that's been interesting him down there in the darkness), and then you hear the chink of his disc, and up the path trots that coal-black shape—our Tam—to hop up the step, that once was too high for him, and into the house, back into the warm, into our midst.

SUNDAY, 30 NOVEMBER

Marianne said to me the other Sunday when we were all about to go for a spin in the car.

"It's unfair to leave him at home, why not take him? After all he's part of the family."

"I can't stand him climbing all over me when I'm trying to drive", I said.

"You're just worried about getting your precious coat dirty," answered Marianne.

—A shrewd thrust, as I *am* fastidious, even squeamish about my clothing. A great handwasher too.

"No, it's not just that."

"Yes, it is", she replies, "I know you well enough by now, and it's such a pity to leave him on his own."

"I draw the line at him putting his mucky paws all over my shoulders when I'm at the wheel. He distracts me."

"The girls can look after him in the back."

"Yes", they say in chorus, "Take him. Go on, Dad!"

"What if he's sick?" I continue.

"What a poor argument! You must be hard pressed, Derek."

"Oh, all right then."

Tam must have been listening. Hardly had Marianne opened the house door—we were standing in the front garden—but he shot out, in through the open car-door and in no time at all there he was, sitting upright on the back seat, like a good boy.

I thought of us children at Elementary School, taught to sit up extra-straight at our desks at a quarter to four, because the best-behaved would be let out early, before the Lord's Prayer.—A fine way to teach religion!

MONDAY, 1 DECEMBER

Of course he sniffs other dogs' bottoms—what dog doesn't?—but curiously, affectionately, yes, courteously, never greedily. Always that dignity about him, a gentleman amongst dogs. Only very occasionally does some other dog's scent displease his nostrils and he'll go for the dog, or vice versa. One of his few pet aversions is a big fat elderly caramel-coloured labrador called Wampums whom he sometimes meets at the Tennis Club opposite. Then the sparks fly. But apart from Wampums whom he often hears in the evening, woof-woofing a few houses down the road (when he'll prick his ears up and give a short sharp bark or two), he has no enemies. Certainly he conducts no feuds. Not like human beings who can be vindictive, even after years of lying low, storing up resentment, to strike at the opportune moment. I've met it, oh yes! and from people who you think would know better. The malice of clever men with too much time on their hands.

In Tam I got to know a creature in whom there was no guile. An Israelite indeed!, for Tam too is swarthy, brown-eyed and quick as a Jew. But not an ounce of calculation in him, that bane of human beings, not a scrap of ill-will, no meanness whatsoever. Instead, such generosity, openness to whatever the moment brings, loyalty.

You can see it immediately in the way he makes himself utterly vulnerable to me or Marianne or the girls—his family—by lying on his back, exposing all his tender parts, to let you rub his belly with the sole of your shoe. "Grovelling by numbers!" I say to him, "Begin", after I've returned home in the course of the afternoon, sometimes lonely and rather disconsolate. I duly rub his tummy, as he wants me to, then up he springs and off into our cloakroom to snatch something. Once the initial reconciliation, as it were, is effected, the bond renewed, he's ready for anything.

And so much of my limited academic life (7 years as a schoolmaster, 13 as a university lecturer), the tangle of my career, the thickets of middle-age I'm fast straying into, the disappointments of human

44

relationships—with the best will in the world (and who possesses that?) how much is flawed in our dealings with each other, and especially at work!, at least this is my finding, and I don't regard myself as anything special—so much of all this is, thanks to Tam, made good in a flash. What a tonic it is to find one of God's creatures so pleased to see you! How vital it is to feel *at home* with people and the other members of God's creation we share our lives with. As I get older this is the feeling I cherish above all others. Goodwill soars beyond all mere cleverness. It brings on others, brings them out instead of putting them down, worsting, worstening them. There is no humour, never mind wisdom or goodness without benevolence. The mystics are right. "Love gets in, where knowledge stands at the door."

So I go and make a cup of tea, give Tam his share of course, then, having switched on the gas-fire in the front room, take up the day's "Times", (that's if the printers are not on strike!) pull my armchair up to the fire, with my back to the light and sip my tea. Tam, having polished off his "cup", joins me. With a sigh he lies down, leaning against my ankles, whence, having warmed himself, he comes to rest under my chair, near me, his master, or rather his fellow, needing the comfort of proximity, the life-giving warmth of companionship (for do we two not share our toast?), security. If you love a woman, you marry her to spend your days with her; if you love a friend you go and see him as often as you can, to be with him. We're all basically gregarious animals. Loneliness is crippling, indeed killing. And how much of the animal is in us all, under the trappings of civilisation!

How better to achieve safety than by snuggling against another warm living being? (In Germany children speak of sleeping close together as "löffelchesweise", like spoons resting one in the other). I can feel right now Tam's heart beating quick against the stockinged sole of my foot.

Sometimes he'll get up, stand by my chair and silently seek to draw my hand from the book I'm reading, to have it stroke his head. Or I'll feel his cold nose trying to nuzzle my palm.

Dear Tam! There's no one quite like you.

FRIDAY, 5 DECEMBER

He puts me in touch with new worlds.

When I go with him to fetch Marianne from the shop at 5.30, all sorts of creatures come to life. First a snappish Afghan Hound just round the corner jumps up fiercely at the high wire-netting as we pass. Then a few doors along comes a border collie, "Sheila", owned by an old lady, both ageing. Sheila greets Tam as an equal. Then there's the little friendly white Cairn Terrier, Tam's favourite, standing at the gate of the Nursing Home, its short stiffish tail going twenty to the dozen at the sight of "the boy". The two dogs sniff each other amiably through the railings of the gate, then first Tam cocks his leg up and pees against a bar, to be followed by his friend who gives a squirt on the same spot. All very decorous.

FRIDAY, 12 DECEMBER

Sometimes he'll fart, always silently (I hasten to add) as he lies by the fire or under one of our armchairs, while we watch television in the evening. An awful stink comes up, but he just lies there, not letting on.

"You been fartin', eh?" asks Elisabeth, with a laugh.

Suddenly I'm reminded of that early morning ride as a boy on a milk-float, accompanying the milkman on his rounds—we were on holiday in Llangollen—when the horse, gleaming in the sun, pulling the cart did exactly the same.

Human propriety, indeed morality, is often so much cant. Take that so-called vitally necessary research, those rows of rhesus monkeys I saw on television tonight, clamped on perches, puffing cigarette-smoke for hours till they dropped, in order to test the tar-content of certain brands. And we use the word "dog" or "ape" as an insult!

FRIDAY, 26 DECEMBER

A friend of mine at the University, and his mother, up from London, came to visit us last night. She's very good-hearted and a great dog-lover.

Of course Tam made a fuss of them as soon as they arrived—any guest of ours is a guest of his. No sooner is she seated on the sofa in the front room but he goes over and starts making up to her. Without a moment's hestitation she picks him up and plonks him onto her lap. He glances at us, as if to say. "Well, what do you think of that, eh?" A treat unheard-of. He knows very well by now he shouldn't get up onto chairs and yet here he is on our guest's lap, and what's more, we can't do anything about it.

You should see the smug look on his face, as he lies there, wallowing, just like a pampered child.

SUNDAY, 28 DECEMBER

Tonight, for some reason, Tam chose to bed down by the back door, leaning against the large "sausage" which keeps out the draught, and which he likes to drag about the house. Catherine had taken an old cushion and put it under his head and laid a fawn cloth over him. There he lay, beautifully tucked in.

As Marianne and I said "goodnight" to him, he hardly opened his eyes, only the bottom of the cloth moved up and down with the wag of his tail.

1.   Tam about three months old.
2.   Princes St. Gardens, Edinburgh.
3.   Catherine, Elisabeth and Tam in the front garden.
4.   The back garden, showing the first and second lawn.
5.   Sam.
6.   Morningside Road, Edinburgh.
7.   Marianne, Catherine, Tam and I relaxing in the back garden.
8.   Tam.

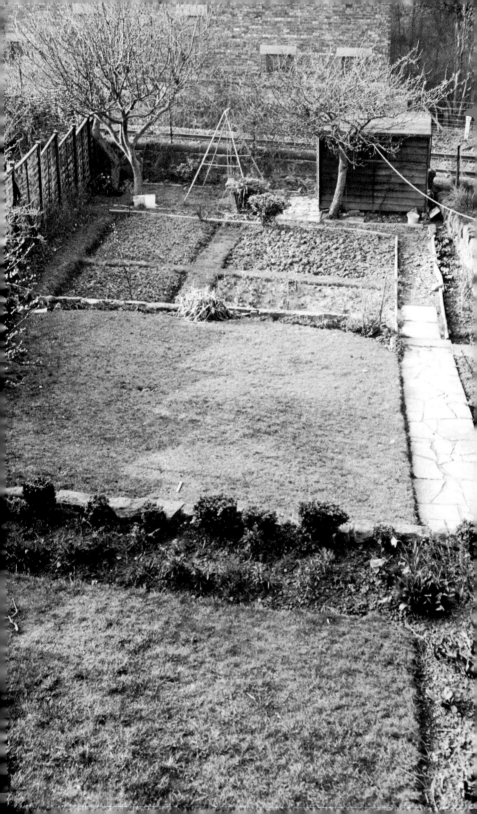

1976

FRIDAY, 2 JANUARY

He may have acute hearing, but I believe it's his sense of smell that he goes by.

Take this morning. After breakfast, I threw out his toast as usual onto our top lawn, which was covered with a few inches of snow. It was so soft that the fragments sank a couple of inches. So there they lay, embedded.

Right! Off Tam goes to the back door. Having let him out, I return to the window. I notice he has the greatest difficulty finding his way to the various pieces. He's sniffing about aimlessly, at a loss. He's been accustomed to following his nose from one piece of toast to another—you can tell this from the way he keeps his head down, tracking—and now the snow gets in his way. It doesn't, allow the smells to emerge, and so he's bound to flounder.

When his nose can operate, it's infallible, even down to the tiniest crumbs I've shaken out of the bread-basket at the window, or scraped off the bread-board at the back door, with him sitting outside, waiting.

Like my father I hold it a sin to burn bread. I don't even like putting it in the bin. The same with paper, if there's ever any waste about the house with a surface blank on it, I stick it in a big paper-clip for further use. Indeed I heartily dislike waste of any kind, but especially of man's staple food, bread. Marianne's the same, but then her father was a master baker. She herself has been baking our bread now for the last three or four years. She couldn't stomach the bread the bakers were selling any longer.

"A bad sign in a culture, once the bread goes. That soggy stuff they offer! Should be ashamed of themselves", she says, "It's like a shortage of good wood. No wonder the currency's rotten."

SUNDAY, 4 JANUARY

I saw this film tonight about jackals in "The World about Us". The puppies were nice enough, but how ghastly the adults!, lying in wait till the tigers had faced all the danger, done all the chasing, struck down the prey, then moving in themselves in a pack. Then that vengefulness. Almost like human beings.

Tam's different, for all they say dogs are descended from wolves. He may have very sharp teeth, but he's not destructive or ferocious. Even during the puppy stage he restricted his attentions to certain things like waste-paper, balls, pegs, slippers and certain mats. He soon realised, or was made to, which were the valuable carpets in the house, and left them studiously alone. Same with books.

Fruit in a bowl on a shelf or low cupboard is perfectly safe, nor has he ever taken any of my pipes which stand in a wooden rack on top of the gas-fire in the front room. Nor does he ever leap up or claw curtains, as cats are prone to do, though he'll steal any gloves or socks going, the latter especially, if they're rolled into a ball or draped in a row over the radiator in our living-room. Then they're irresistible to him.

He's no danger to children, or grown-ups for that matter. You can leave him with complete confidence in the same room with a baby. The disadvantage is he's no use as a guard-dog. If any thief entered, he'd simply lie on his back, waiting for him to tickle his tummy.

Well, you can't have it all ways.

FRIDAY, 23 JANUARY

Marianne and I went to a concert at the Usher Hall this evening. On the way back we called in at The Globetrotter along Bruntsfield Place and bought three fish suppers (40p each) for us, the girls and "the boy". Very partial to a fish supper, he is. He can always tell the moment we enter the house, that we've been eating fish and chips, even if we don't bring any home. But if we bring back any portions, then there's no stopping him.

Well, this time the girls quickly got out plates, knives and forks and I put the kettle on. I've long held the view that fish and chips are best consumed with a good hot cup of tea—helps melt the fat. As for Tam, he was like a creature possessed. He must have his, and pronto! So I took a handful of chips out of each packet, pulled off some of the fish in batter, and put it all in his bowl in the kitchen. He set to with a vengeance. The lot was wolfed down in ten seconds flat. Then, while we were eating our portions in the livingroom he sat there by me, straight-backed, intent, making his hunger felt to all and sundry, *willing* us to give him more.

"All right, Tam," I said "Come on, into the kitchen. Here's your afters", and put a few more chips into his bowl. Ah!, that rich smell of fried haddock and delicious chips, that mixture of hot fat and the sharp tang of vinegar.

Then came the noise of him lapping up his tea from the margarine container in the kitchen. We couldn't help smiling.

THURSDAY, 19 FEBRUARY

When Tam gets an itch, say in the middle of walking across the room, he'll suddenly collapse in a heap, utterly given over to scratching the offending place, whether it be under his crotch or behind his ears. "Whump! Whump! Whump!" goes his paw, as he works away with extreme vigour and concentration. Then that done, relieved, he'll get up and resume his progress, as if nothing had happened.

Whatever he does, it engages his whole being. Like the Germans in this—they never do things by halves.

FRIDAY, 20 FEBRUARY

Let's face it, he's not always easy. The difficulty in rearing him lies in restricting his movement. I watched him this morning from Elisabeth's bedroom window, standing with his forepaws on the garden-wall between our property and our neighbour's. There he was at the bottom of the garden, which slopes down towards the railway. He's obviously yearning to get up and over, but undecided whether to risk it, for he's glancing towards the house to see if we're watching.

I *know* he occasionally hops over. He's now fully grown and has no difficulty getting down the other side, as there's a pile of soil and rubbish there. Nevertheless it's not easy to catch him playing truant. I believe he goes over under cover of darkness. He certainly needs plenty of elbow-room—thank goodness for the garden!

That's the trouble. You can't keep tabs on him the whole time.

SUNDAY, 9 MARCH

We've been getting a lot of birds in our back garden lately, now there's a bit of heat in the sun again—not much, but enough. Tam likes to sit and watch them (after he's had his toast). I've always maintained he has an essentially peaceable nature.

All sorts frequent the top lawn, as we have a bird-house in the middle and regularly fill a red net hanging from it with pea-nuts, or scatter breadcrumbs, bacon-rinds etc. onto the grass. We get starlings—lots of them, chattering and fussing—sparrows, of course, finches of all kinds (very fierce *they* are, mind you, the male black-birds take a lot of beating), thrushes, robins—little beauties, aren't they?—crows, even a hooded crow—the latter's been lurking round our place for a number of years now. Sometimes, when it's stormy, seagulls come, but they have great difficulty landing. And high up in the sky, flocks of geese, continually adjusting on the wing the living shape of their flights, and ducks, often in pairs. How wonderfully they wheel and veer so close together! And so low you can hear their wings flap.

A whole parliament of birds then, vociferous, as all parliaments are.

There he'll sit, Tam, at the top of the garden, on the flags (covered with old chalk marks where Catherine and her friends have been playing hopscotch), upright, sniffing the morning air, enjoying life, as always. Watching these odd little fellow-creatures flitting about, hopping, scrapping, alighting on our willows and apple-trees or on the neighbour's ash and lilac, where they "sing among the branches" or flutter across to sit pert on the fence. Oops! a little fresh white dropping slips from one as it flies through the air.

He sits there absorbed, even if it's so windy his coat ruffles. He doesn't stir. He never chases them mischievously. He may earlier today have cleared some off the lawn, but that was because of his toast. Nor is he interested in pursuit. No, he just sits there, *appreciating* them, these fellow creatures, fluttering and chirruping, gathering straw and twigs for nests, mating, feeding, fighting, pulling up elastic worms, after hopping about the lawn with their heads on one side close to the ground, listening for them there in our garden. After all, what is better than appreciating the here and now, taking it in affectionately, fully?— Goethe's great lesson in "The Italian Journey", as in so many of his writings. Children do so instinctively, geniuses work at it, saints attain this attitude of clear-sighted innocence. Of course there was no thought of proprietorship on Tam's part—that was half, or more, of his secret. Isn't that what makes a man vulgar—when he can't see something beautiful and cherish it without wanting to own it?

Some of our neighbours do seem to need an awful lot of big things. And even when they have them, they're grumpy. Take the University. Even knowledge, thanks to degrees, is all too often regarded as a commodity. I'm always a trifle suspicious of anyone who has a string of letters after his name. It's as if the man himself needs propping up.

Nevertheless by that time of day Tam had a full belly, and that helps—I can't remember him ever leaving any toast on the lawn, no matter how much we threw out. If we wanted the birds to get any, we simply had to "confine him to barracks".

How amusing it is for Marianne and me, both of us in our forties, for the first time dog-owners after a shaky start, to sit at the breakfast-table, once the girls have gone off to school, and watch Tam's black head move to left and right, like a spectator at Wimbledon, or up and down, as his gaze follows the various birds. It's as good as a cabaret.

SATURDAY, 28 MARCH

We've got some old friends from Liverpool staying with us for the weekend. They came up last night on a flying visit to attend a Jewish

Wedding on Sunday. This evening we gave a dinner for them.

Already by late afternoon, as Marianne was getting things ready, Tam was aware of something in the air. Always the same with him. When the guests at last arrived, he wanted to jump up—this black whirlwind of ours—and greet each one with due warmth, but instead, oh dear!, he now found himself confined to his box in the kitchen.

Why do we have to keep him out?

Later during the meal, through all the conversation, I kept thinking of him. In the end, when I went to the kitchen for dessert dishes, you should have seen him lying there, black as the ace of spades, in his now so battered cardboard box (we've looked at various dog-baskets in our time, but we're afraid he'll still grow out of them), his thin longish bony head resting over the side, gazing up sadly. As I opened the cabinet, I could feel those great brown eyes following my every move. I put down the dishes, went over to him, bent down and stroked him. Immediately that bushy tail started slapping the sides of his box. Was it relief that at least I wasn't angry with him? I got up to return to my guests and, as I closed the door behind me, I could hear him sigh. I re-entered my other world.

When later on, by special request, he was allowed into the front room, he entered bashfully, and only after mutedly greeting each person in turn, with just his tail registering something of the warmth of his feelings, was he ready to lie down in front of the fire and allow everything to proceed around him. He sensed he had to be on his best behaviour. Now that he'd seen who these friends of ours were (and our friends were his of course), and what we were all doing, he was content. He wasn't going to force his attentions on us, he knew better.

Yes, that was the right atmosphere, convivial, if measured.

MONDAY, 5 APRIL

These last few days Marianne's been ill in bed with 'flu which is doing its rounds again, so I've been looking after "the boy", with the help of the girls. He's obviously been missing her, from the way he's been silently sitting at the foot of the stairs.

This morning I took Tam upstairs with me as a special treat. As soon as he got the O.K., he trotted up, raced across the landing, and jumped up at Marianne, sitting up in bed, her cashmere shawl over her pyjamas. She stroked his head and he sat there at the bedside, looking up at her from time to time, while I talked to her.

When we came downstairs, he couldn't resist barking and snapping playfully at my heels, tangling himself a bit in my legs. He was glad, even grateful, to have paid his visit.

THURSDAY, 15 APRIL

We don't often chastise him now—he doesn't seem to need it. Not that we ever did much, but when I think of this time last year! There *is* such a thing as progress, only you don't often notice it at the time. It's like your children growing up.

Yesterday I struck him in anger—he stole some of my seed potatoes, chewed them, then left them. The shock upset him. Marianne has shouted at him much more often than I. Such a blow coming from me hurt him, I do believe, more than if it had come from her.

Once we've established our system, he's generally ready to abide by it, and when he infringes it, is shame-facedly prepared to take his medicine. It's true, that phrase, "a hang-dog look". Like today when he got out and went over to the other side of the road. I was looking out of the bay-window at the time and could hardly believe my eyes.— Rather disturbing, this "Wanderlust" of his. I gave him what for, though, once he was safely back in our front garden, but I had to be careful how I caught him, as Cluny Gardens is a busy road.

Marianne and I were just talking about this; she's really afraid he might cause an accident.

One of the interesting things about rearing a dog is how far to go with discipline. Of course Tam's constantly having to stomach new doses of our "regime", new rules he must abide by, and occasionally he does disobey, at times insistently. I sometimes think the apparent arbitrariness of our behaviour does surprise and upset him, till he comes to accept it. On the whole he's an apt pupil, but he must have thought to himself more than once, as he lay there in the kitchen in disgrace, "Rum creatures, these human beings!"

FRIDAY, 14 MAY

Tam had his "booster" today at the "Dick Vet". Marianne tells me he conducted himself with all his customary dignity. A bit subdued since, I've noticed. He was especially pleased to see me when I got back from University late this afternoon. His next injection's due in exactly one year.

So far they seem to have been successful; he's hardly suffered a day's illness. In fact, apart from rainy days which get him down, he's brimming over with health. I wish I had his zip.

He's only been sick on the floor a few times. When he is, he makes a point of returning to his vomit and licking it up. He performs this operation quietly and carefully, without the least sign of disgust. Rather convenient for us. He's been sick more often in the garden than indoors, and especially on the paths between our four vegetable patches down at the bottom near the apple-trees. Being sick like this doesn't seem to upset him unduly, rather like small children.

On the top lawn there are still brown patches from where he's been in the habit of peeing. The acid, I suppose. Nowadays, however, he especially favours the red-hot poker and the rhododendron with his attentions.

TUESDAY, 18 MAY

I've been doing a spot of gardening lately. These Victoria Day Holidays are a splendid institution—bless the regal memory! Tam with me of course. A great help, I must say!, particularly if I'm pricking out plants. He's fascinated, and whenever I have seedlings, bulbs or corms beside me, and I'm kneeling, busy with the trowel, he's liable to slink up, snatch one or two and pelt off. Well, he's not getting a chase. There's too much to do, so I give him a good clout.

He's a bit put out at the harshness of my reaction, when really he has no right to be—he knows perfectly well he's been doing wrong. He could easily ruin the plants. We can't have that! After chastisement, he lies down doggo in the soil or on top of the montbretias, giving me a wide berth; I call it sulking. Then after a bit, he wanders off unconcerned.

He's still chary of rose-bushes; he pricked himself badly once. I can still see him with the blood flowing dark red, then so quickly sticking in his jet black hair. It soon became a light brown crust on his coat, like dried mud.

WEDNESDAY, 19 MAY

I've just come in from an afternoon walk. I need a rest, I'm telling you!

The way he has to pee, or try to, against any old lamp-post!, pulling you this way and that, to go and cock his leg up against a gate-post or bush and give it a squirt. Where he gets it all from is anyone's guess! By the allotments up Midmar Drive it's tufts of tussocky grass that get him going—they must be full of the scent of many a dog, as it's a favourite route for dog-walkers. But along a road it's lamp-posts, gate-posts, creosoted fences etc.

Of course he sniffs at other dog's droppings, as well as his own. What dog doesn't? But there's no trace of prurience about him, such as you find in human beings, never mind "the frigid villainy of studied lewdness", as the great Dr Johnson terms it. Again that innocence of his.

When you take him for a walk, he usually does his business twice. On the first occasion his dung is hard, on the second softer, more yellowish, at times so soft it drips out. From his faeces one can immediately see what he's been eating. As a puppy he tried to eat anything he could possibly get his teeth into—toys, Tupperware, plastic bowls and plates, scraps of material, cleaning rags, rugs, carpets. Then, as one might expect, the stuff showed in his dung, with the original colours remaining in patches—red, yellow, white, blue. If Tam had been chewing string or cord, some of it might well hang inside dung from his bottom, and he'd find it difficult to drop it. He'd get most upset, trying at all costs to shake it or swing it off—he didn't like to apply his mouth near—and would stop every few feet to twist and turn in order somehow to rid himself of this upsetting appendage, like an academic worrying a vexed question. Once he did succeed he'd walk on, immensely relieved. The article had at last come out!

THURSDAY, 20 MAY

I was talking about how clean and proper the boy is. Yes, his bottom is always perfectly clean, and it's hidden under hair, unlike poodles, for instance. But we don't seem to be able to train him to do his business in the gutter. This can offend pedestrians, and quite rightly so.

SATURDAY, 22 MAY

I spoke too soon about his cleanliness. He simply can't resist fresh horse manure.

I was walking along Blackford Glen Road—nice afternoon (makes a change from tennis)—and had just passed Blackford Quarry when he came across a pile of the stuff, still steaming, in the road. Unfortunately he was off his lead at the time (it's a quiet road). Well, first he takes a good deep sniff, then turns his right shoulder into it, bends and rolls himself right down in it. I couldn't believe my eyes. Wallowing in it. The job I had, getting his lead on and dragging him away! He even growled at me. Ugh!, he stank to high heaven. I couldn't wait to get him home and bath him—he doesn't like that, not one bit.

I now know what we mean when we say "dirty dog". That's not the first expression to do with dogs that I've come to understand with a new vividness, since we got Tam. Our proverbs are nearly always spot on, our language is so much wiser than we are individually.

SUNDAY, 23 MAY

I will say this for Elisabeth—she's really been trying to train Tam several months now on her regular Sunday morning pre-prandial walks with him down the Hermitage of Braid (a favourite stamping-ground for dogs). "Come to heel," "Walk", "Stop" etc. With the aid of Polos of course—you can't achieve anything without inducements of one sort or another. But she's had little success. He only has to glimpse another dog and off he pelts. They do say males are the worst. I also suppose it's the sheep-dog in him. Perhaps he'll slow down with age—*I* have—well, let's hope so.

THURSDAY, 26 MAY

As I may have mentioned—Tam, like me, has to have a hot cup of tea with his fish-supper. Weak, with lots of milk and not too hot. He can't take coffee, and as for other beverages, we've never tried cocoa on him, or any alcohol—that would have been asking for trouble! And doesn't he gollop his tea down from his container! Then to round off the performance he thrusts his nose deep into it, like Eric Morecambe's imitation of Schnozzle Durante, and belts the light plastic object round the kitchen, trying to suck the goodness out of every cranny. Frustrating, as he can't get a proper purchase on it.

"Pity he can't turn it inside out!" says Marianne. Looking at him, I'm suddenly reminded of the little kids at Ranworth Square Elementary School years ago (I was one), sucking the last ounce of goodness out of their small fat thick-glassed milk-bottles. All those empty vessels resounding from different quarters in the classroom. The straws were made of real straw in those days.

Yes, a great drinker, the boy. Always liked his milk too, when he was smaller. But now it's tea. He knows what's good for him.

TUESDAY, 1 JUNE

He's always loved children right from the very start. You should have seen him as we proceeded down Comiston Road, when I took him for a walk at mid-day! We came to South Morningside School, and there they were!, all those children, laughing, shouting, running and playing football in the schoolyard, several games criss-crossing.

As soon as we were past the first gate, which has a barrier in front of it to stop children from darting out into the street, he strained at the leash, jumped up at the railings, then, with his forepaws firmly planted on the low coping stone, insisted on staring at it all, his hair ruffling in the wind, his ears flicking, his tail wagging furiously, all agog. He started barking—how could he help it?—and some of the children came towards him. He thrust his paw between the railings for them, and let his face be stroked. No fear, he'd never bite. He wasn't like that. If only he were allowed in, let loose amongst these marvellous youngsters, of which he was one, *he'd* show them! He'd dash and jump and chase about everywhere in that yard with the best of them. I could feel the tug of him on his lead, like a kite, urging, thrusting up into the sky.

I had to give him a couple of minutes at least, even though I had to get back in time for lunch. Then I pulled him, indeed hauled him down and along with me—he would insist on craning sideways the whole time, standing on his back legs. And then, when we went past the second gates, he dug in his heels and I had to drag him, slithering along the pavement. Passers-by were smiling. I thought of when I was in the Boys' Brigade at our weekly evening meeting in a school in Walton, Liverpool, and the Captain of the Company would complain,

"I won't have these bits of girls hanging around the school-gates, waiting for you lads to come out. Like so many bees round a honey-pot."

—The distaste with which he mouthed his sentiments. Some people do find natural instincts difficult to accept.

At last Tam relented. Only once or twice as we continued down Comiston Road did he wistfully glance round. But he'll never forget that school.

SATURDAY, 5 JUNE

I don't know whether it's because I'm excited about the prospect of a plane journey to Lüneburg—I hate flying, I have too much imagination—or whether I'm nervous of the reception such a highly critical audience will give my paper there, but I've been sleeping badly. I envy Tam the way he can snooze, and yet it would be wrong to call him lazy.

The truth is, he can, like a snake, combine alertness and relaxation. As for us human beings, only perhaps a mother in bed with a baby sleeping nearby, knows this state. Only she can both rest and be watchful.

On such occasions Tam flattens himself to the ground. Often he chooses the hall—and not only because of the patches of sunlight there (our front door is glass-panelled), but also to keep an eye on as many things as possible. Take an ordinary Saturday, like this morning. Marianne is busy hoovering out the hall, Catherine cleaning the shoes in the cloakroom by the back door and Elisabeth and I washing up in the kitchen, with the door open that leads into the hall. Tam has taken up position a yard or so from the front door, facing into the house. There, from his observation post, flat out, forepaws extended, eyes hooded, he can immediately register and is poised to respond to any move. Deans are like this in Faculty Offices, I've noticed.

I've also seen sheep-dogs at a sheep-trial lie exactly the same way in a field, as they motionlessly guide, indeed *will,* their charges along

58

towards the gate they have to go through. The silly sheep may then flounder or bolt; immediately the dog shoots ahead to check them, obeying the shepherd's whistle.

—Again that sheep-dog instinct in him. The older he gets, the more it comes out. I wonder sometimes if he wouldn't have been happier in the wild.

SUNDAY, 6 JUNE

This morning, while I was doing a bit of sketching, Catherine took Tam up Midmar Drive, past the allotments to a sheep field. No sheep there, I hasten to add. She lets him off his leash, whereupon he goes and rolls in sheep-droppings. Whether the wasps were already in the dung or not, whatever the case, this attracted a number of them. They got embedded in his thick coat, buzzing there and stinging him; panicky themselves, no doubt. Catherine picked out all those she could, getting stung herself for her pains. They arrived home, both highly agitated.

Of course "the boy" had to have a bath, something he doesn't relish even at the best of times. He's lying in his box in the kitchen at the moment, dried and powdered white, all sorry for himself. He looks a right sight. Catherine's right hand has come up like a suet pudding.

No lack of incident with that boy around!

WEDNESDAY, 9 JUNE
LÜNEBURG; HOTEL AM PARK

Attending the Hamann Conference here. Yesterday evening I was lonely in my hotel room. I thought of Tam that first night nearly two years ago, crying in our kitchen hour after hour, poor little thing. We all need the easing, the comfort of company. Our spiky individuality gets us down; we're inadequate, wretched on our own.

Tonight in conversation with an expert on Hamann—a fine man— I recalled that first night when Tam arrived under our roof and Marianne covered a hot water bottle and laid him against it. Thinking it was his mother, he snuggled up against it, against *her,* stopped crying and dropped off, comforted.

"We all seek such consolation" I said, "in this terrifying universe we've been flung into. It *is* terrifying—you've only got to step out of your house on a winter's night and stand in the dark for awhile to realise it."

"Yes," he said, "We're all like that puppy. Acquaintance, friendship, love, marriage, religion—they're all part of that same search for ultimate security. Remember St Augustine's words?—'Thou hast made us for Thyself and our hearts are restless until they find their rest in Thee.' That in essence was what your Tam was after, and good luck to him, I say."

SATURDAY, 26 JUNE

Back home. Much warmer now. Right menagerie we've got here!

Leaving Tam aside for the moment, you should see the guinea-pig out there in the back garden, now the weather's fine! We've made a pen or ranch for Sam on our second lawn. In the morning, for several weeks now, one of the girls and I have lugged his wooden box out into the garden with him inside, chunnering away. There he'll stay for the day if it's fine.

His box is so constructed that the frontage is largely taken up by a door of wire mesh, held at the bottom by a catch; it lifts up and out to open. On the right is a small wooden door which slides up. Inside, Sam's box is lined as follows: first layer, a plastic bag; second, a folded newspaper (generally *The Scotsman*), or the *Radio Times,* then comes sawdust and finally Sweet Meadow Hay from Dofo's, the pet shop along Morningside Road.

How Sam loves his box when Marianne's cleaned it out and it's freshly garnished! When the newspaper and sawdust and old hay, soggy with urine and sprinkled with several days' droppings are removed, Tam is never far away, there are so many goodies to snaffle.

"Right. Come on, Sam. Into the box with you!" she says, and the guinea-pig, who's been lurking about outside, clambers up (that funny fat rump of his, lumbering up the step of half an inch) and nestles down right inside the sweet-smelling cosy fresh stuff, digging himself in, as Trudie our tortoise used to do in his pile of mulch. How he rustles away there, till he's entirely surrounded by hay and huddled up into a ball, so you can no longer see him, safe and snug there in the warm. Nothing like it!

Sam has a fawn water bowl, about the size of a small cup, only flat underneath, also a dark-brown plastic feeding-bowl of a similar size for his "Pip" (the guinea-pig food). Sometimes he tramples on the water bowl, dirtying it, or he'll blunder into it, knocking it over. I don't think he sees very well, and he's not only clumsy but also a bit on the slow side (intellectually, I mean), though he knows which side his bread is buttered on. He recognises, for instance, certain sounds about the house and duly responds. When anyone opens the pantry door, then he's liable to start gnawing at the mesh of his cage, producing an annoying rattle. This opening of the pantry-door is no doubt associated in his mind with carrots, to which he is very partial.

His cage is lodged in different places during the course of the year. Over the winter it's in the cloakroom, spring and autumn the front porch, and in the summer, weather permitting, the garden.

Well, this morning, since it was fine, Catherine and I duly carried him out to the second lawn, then set him down with the back of his box against the middle of the low stone wall that makes up the end of the first terrace. There he can get both sunshine and shelter, the only snag being that he can't move about and enjoy the sunshine.

Catherine said "Why don't we get some chicken-wire and make a run for him? You promised." "All right" I said, "Let's do that." So we drove to W. Scott and Sons, Nurserymen, along Newington Road, and I bought a small roll of foot-high chicken-wire. While I was there, I couldn't resist buying a couple of clematis for the little trellis at the front of the house between the porch and the bay-window. Back home, I took a few canes from the shed, sawed them in half and stuck them into the lawn, pegging out the corners of Sam's territory, then drew the chicken-wire round them.

Once the run was safe and stoutly fixed (or so we thought), I lifted up Sam's larger front door and tied it with string to a branch of the willow that grows nearby (the one I once worried over, thinking I'd cut it back too drastically). Now the little fellow can come and go as he pleases. Besides his water and his guinea-pig food, Marianne or the girls give him extra tit-bits, such as leaves of lettuce, dandelion or cabbage (his beloved "greens"), a carrot or a piece of swede.

—So now he's in his element.

THURSDAY, 1 JULY

It's only two yards square, if that, Sam's private territory in the garden, but no matter how we try, we can't get Tam to respect it. Mind you, I suppose we should be grateful for small mercies—at least he doesn't attack him. I like to think this tolerance is a result of the training we've given the two animals over the last few months, accustoming them to each other, making a fuss of Tam whenever he seemed to be getting jealous. But however hard we try to keep Tam out of Sam's patch, we fail; he simply will not heed. No good shouting at him or even hitting him with a rolled-up newspaper, as I did this afternoon. Chase him out over the chicken-wire, and as soon as your back's turned, he'll hop back over that diminutive fence and stand there quietly, sniffing about in the meadow-hay, snaffling Sam's pieces of apple or anything else available. No scuffles, though, over food—Sam keeps back—nor does he harm the guinea-pig in any way.

I repeat, he doesn't stay there provocatively. He never *flaunts* his authority; he merely asserts it. He's demonstrating that he belongs there every bit as much as Sam, indeed as anybody. The garden is his domain as well as ours or Sam's, and of course, he has a perfect right to it when all's said and done. He's not greedy in this—not like that blackbird I saw the other day with its mouth already crammed with food, attacking another bird for more. Tam doesn't have what I call "the hog at the trough mentality" which, I'm afraid, I've observed in various human beings, sometimes ones who should know better.

Anyway, what do we own in this life, when it comes down to it? Everything's only entrusted to us. Our very souls belong not to ourselves, but to God.

SATURDAY, 3 JULY

Sam—the little devil!—has been interfering with his fence again. I went out after lunch to have a look at him. Gone! And the chicken-wire lifted and buckled! It was the same last Monday. I found him in amongst the flowers by the elder tree. Having a rare old time he was, rooting about, nibbling any shoot or stalk in sight!

I grabbed him, plonked him down in his ranch and watched. Hardly back inside, he scuttled to the fence, bent his head down, grabbed at the mesh near the bottom and wrenched it upwards and inwards with his strong little teeth (in the same way that he gnaws the door of his box). Talk about persistence! Then the fence, once loosened, he shouldered it up, and in an instant he'd flattened himself under it as well as he could with his chubby figure, then whoosh! out. Bionic pig with a vengeance! for all the shortness of his legs. I bought staples and hammered them into the soil to try to get it to stay put, but they're of little use.

Today he's amongst the flowers again. I only hope he doesn't get it into his little head to slip under the fence between the gardens— "Well, back into your ranch you go."

Tam's also partial to skulking amongst the flowers and shrubs that have grown up thick in the bed there. But he's not after succulent shoots like Sam. He'll hide there when he's having a chase, or dash down behind the plants. At other times he'll lie flat, watchful, on top of the clumps of strap-leaved montbretia about the garden, his favourites (grow anywhere, that will!), rather as a hare will on his form out in a field.

How smartly Sam nips for cover, whether on the lawn or on the carpet in our living room! He hates to be exposed. Tam loves it. Of course Sam's much more timid than "the boy", which is only to be expected of such a little animal, with so many dangers, often potentially fatal, lurking everywhere. I've begun to realise how fear in all its different forms also plays an often hidden part in human behaviour. Greed, exploitation, manipulation of others, can be a form of panic.

SUNDAY, 4 JULY

It's now absolutely impossible to catch Tam in the garden. It never was easy, now it's out of the question. Even if Elisabeth and I finally succeed in cornering him down under the apple-trees, he'll still dart away like greased lightning. If I'm serious about catching him I can get angry, as I did a year ago, when on the shore at Aberlady Bay, I found I simply couldn't catch Elisabeth (she was 14 at the time). I'd been so used to feeling automatically her athletic superior, just as a teacher feels intellectually superior when he asks his pupils questions, the answers to which he already knows. But human beings are just not in the same league with Tam when it comes to nimbleness.

Then off he goes with whatever he happens to have between his teeth. It doesn't matter what it is—that's not the point. All he wants is a chase. It's a bit like the rat-race at work—with degrees and publications and promotion, substituted for rags, slippers, ball—only, as opposed to the deadly seriousness with which academics tend to pursue their careers, in Tam's case there's a splendid elation, exhilaration about the game. Here in our back garden this dog of ours displays a sophistication little known within the groves of academe.

This afternoon it was hot and we were sitting out under our willow-tree. Marianne must have spent a good hour trying to get "the boy" actually to fetch his ball, bring it and drop it voluntarily out of his jaws. He did come nearer and nearer with it, he even lay down at her feet, but every time she went to take the ball off him he instinctively recoiled. In the end since neither she nor I would get up, Tam slumped under Marianne's deck chair, panting, mouth wide-open, tongue hanging out, fed up with the whole stupid business.

He wouldn't learn. Well, why should he? Who was being stubborn, Tam or us?

TUESDAY, 6 JULY

He knows and, if necessary, establishes and defends his rights, such as the choice of where to lie at night or where to stay in the house if we go out, leaving him on his own. It's been obvious from early on that he hates being confined to the kitchen on such occasions, but only during the last few months has he acted on this dislike of his.

As soon as he noticed we were getting ready to go to bed or go out, he would take up position under the sofa or gramophone table in the front room (if the door was open) or under the chair in the hall, or, at a pinch, under the sideboard in the living-room—always *under* something, and there defend tooth and nail his right to stay and have the run of downstairs. I can't give the exact date when he started this habit, but it's only comparatively recently. It would, however, be wrong to term such behaviour aggressiveness. He's merely establishing his territory, his rights, which is no bad thing in any creature, human beings included. I admire a man who won't allow himself to be put upon.

63

We've established by now a "modus vivendi" with Tam. Since we've been reasonably insistent, he knows pretty well where he is with us four. We've never taken him onto our lap, for instance, neither has he ever been allowed to jump up and sit on our chairs, nor go upstairs, never mind get onto the beds. Once these restrictions on his freedom of movement were made clear to him, he's nearly always obeyed. Only once or twice of late, however, when we've come back home and entered the house unexpectedly we've caught him quickly, furtively jumping down off an armchair, where no doubt he's just been enjoying a rare old snooze, with the knowledge that such behaviour is forbidden, to add that extra spice to his pleasure.

But as I've said all along, he's not a truculent dog. There's no vicious streak in him. He'll always see reason; he's docile, indeed touchingly eager to please, so it's no good whatsoever coming down on him like a ton of bricks, if you don't agree with what he's doing. There's usually a good reason behind it. Anyway you just crush him— well, at least momentarily. The only thing I'm sometimes afraid of is that he may stray one day. He needs plenty of space, lots of activity. Really he's very much the working dog at heart.

THURSDAY, 8 JULY

We're off tomorrow touring England and Wales for a fortnight or so, staying with friends and relations.

Tam quiet last night, didn't even protest about going into his box, as if he knew what was in the offing—kennels.

Terribly hot. I woke up a couple of times during the night and heard him sigh. And once when I went to the lavatory, I heard a half-growl from him as if he were being disturbed by bad dreams. Mind you, Catherine had been feeding him on all sorts of things, including a great hunk of Canadian Cheddar.

I took him in the car to the kennels this morning. We went alone, the girls couldn't face it, said they were too busy packing. I can't say I was enthusiastic myself, but what can you do? I can't inflict "the boy" on friends. Let's face it, he *is* a handful. What friends I have, I can't afford to lose. Not at my age.

MONDAY, 26 JULY

Very hot, even early on. Drove down to the Borders (Tam's country) to fetch "the boy".

Fine this time; I was amazed. Apparently he's had this companion in his cage, it seems to have done the trick. Whether male or female, the girl "wouldn't like to say". That twinkle in her eye. And what a splendid Hertfordshire accent she had! Real countrified. How roguish that "say" of hers sounded! She's new, you can tell; thoroughly enjoys her work too, which is as it should be.

"I only know" she says, bending down to pat Tam on his small head, whereupon his tail starts sweeping the path like a horizontal windscreen wiper, "He seems to have enjoyed every minute of it. Great lad, your Tam!"

Well, knowing Tam, there's bound to be issue—he's a big boy now.

No, this time there was no need for him to recuperate. I still see him sitting there next to me in the car on the way back, as large as life and twice as lively. Had a rare old time, no doubt, every bit as good as ours, thank you very much.

TUESDAY, 27 JULY

I was thinking, yes, it would be an awful shame for Tam's strain, however mongrel, to die out. But why the concessive: "however mongrel"? After all, they say hybrids and bastards make the healthiest specimens—Dame Nature's never averse to a bit of sport. I believe she prefers the bloods to be mixed. Variety's the spice of life.

I shall never be a dog-fancier, just as Tam's not a show dog, and it's right that way!

THURSDAY, 29 JULY

This drought's getting us all down, Tam especially. I feel so sorry for him, flopped out in the shade of the willow-tree for hours at a time, fit for nothing. All his appetite gone. Drink, drink, drink—that's all he does!

SATURDAY, 31 JULY

This afternoon went for a walk with Tam along Hermitage Dell—it's cool down there, under all those great trees. We come to a pool by a waterfall in the Braid Burn. Tam, off his lead, sees two young cocker spaniels, splashing away in the shallows. He rushes into the water on impulse.

My!, does he start back at the coldness of the water. He doesn't like water as it is. I suppose it was a combination of the weather and the enjoyment of those spaniels that made him go in. He emerges pronto, looking a sorry sight and shakes himself violently. We stand well back.

We've hardly ever bathed him, only once or twice, when he's rolled in horse-manure. And then the time when Marianne was doing a spot of decorating and he upset the tin of green emulsion. What a sight he was! We had to use turpentine and I don't know what else. He was licking himself for weeks. After a bath or being out in the rain, he can't wait to be rubbed down with his own towel. It's kept under the stairs and he always hangs about there till we take it out and dry him. He'd never make a gun-dog.

MONDAY, 9 AUGUST

Yesterday afternoon, glorious weather, wonderful light, everything intensely sharp. Marianne, Catherine, Tam and I went for a walk from Colinton across to the Reservoirs and back.

First we had a picnic at the top of the hill, looking down at Bonaly Tower, then out over Edinburgh across the two bridges, new and old, over the Forth to the Fife coast and the hills beyond. Shadows of clouds were sliding across the landscape, everything moved in the wind, even the bracken we sat among, not to mention Tam's coat. Tam crouched in amongst us, busy gobbling any sandwiches going, guzzling his tea out of his container, and crunching a Polo or two to round off the meal.

Then away we strode across the countryside, the three of us, with Tam rushing on ahead, leading the way, barking and foraging in the heather. A burst of speed, and then he'd stop to look back and reassure himself we were still near. Of course he was quite safe up there. He'd return to us, then suddenly pelt off, wanting a chase as usual, then after a while, seeing there was nothing doing, come and trot along at our side.

There's so much of the sheep-dog in him it worries me sometimes. The truth is, now he's grown up, he *needs* the discipline of work, needs his sheep to control, his shepherd to heed. Sometimes, when I see him in the garden, or by the allotments or out in the open country like yesterday, I think of a motor engine racing, never engaging. He may play along for a while, meeting our demands—he does *so* like to please, but essentially he refuses to be trammelled, to be bound by us, for what we do, however attractive it may be at times, is basically frivolous. Our demands are not serious enough. I'm reminded of the old Goethe, recovering from a serious illness, stiffening his resolve to be at his writing-desk early the next morning to resume his life-long literary quest—*"morgen wieder 'ad laborem'"*, back to work tomorrow. That's what Tam needs—to be controlled by duty. I've long loved the wildness in him—what I admire most in people is spirit, mettle—but if he doesn't watch out, one day it'll be the death of him.

Yesterday, however, Tam was in his element with us three whom he loves and feels safe with, running free in the country not so far north from the area where his ancestors had roamed for centuries—the Borders.

Then something happened we'd not bargained for. There were sheep there! The other side of Torduff Hill he sighted them. Away he pelted in pursuit, crazed, chasing now one, now the other, his blood in a blaze of excitement. The poor silly sheep went dashing across the unequal terrain on their little hoofs with him in close pursuit, barking at them, worrying them. What could we do? He was completely removed from us. Centuries of tradition were impelling him, age-old instincts driving him to round those creatures up. He and they were made for each other, he could no more resist that instinct than stop breathing.

Now I chased after him up hill, down dale, shouting after him the whole time, watching I didn't stumble into the many little gullies hidden under the heather, getting more and more out of breath, sweating. He didn't pay the slightest attention. Catherine followed behind, shouting "Tam, Tam, to heel!" Marianne, away in the distance, stood watching.

I was afraid of a brush with the law, what if a farmer or shepherd were suddenly to appear? We'd seen the notices about sheep-worrying.

Well, after several minutes—no longer, but it seemed an age—at last he slowed down and finally allowed me to catch up and put his lead on. His mouth was slavering—a rare thing with Tam—and he was panting, his tongue protruding. But he'd had a run for his money, that was the thing. No shame, why should he feel ashamed? None of the sheep were harmed.

He'd had enough. Of course it would have been a different matter if he'd *really* been rounding up those sheep. He could then have gone on for as long as ever his master required. I've heard of those sheep-dogs at a trial running themselves into the ground, the heart finally giving out from exhaustion. But that would have been work; this was sport. Enough's enough.

He was as good as gold on his leash now, looking up pleasantly at me from time to time as he trotted along at my side, grateful for that brief atavistic spell, that tingling in the marrow, that taste of blood, a return to the old ways he knew he was born for. For all our domestication of him, his being "a good boy" was so much gloss. The call of the wild was in him, and yet it would be unjust to underestimate the bond between us. He did look to us, we were in charge of him.

How he did enjoy himself with us, that afternoon, and in so doing, enriched the experience for us. All those smells, all those different surfaces and textures—grass, gorse, reeds, heather, the bracken, the runnels and gulleys, so dry from the long drought, running down to the brook at the bottom, the grained earth, that freshly exposed black soil and orange clay where an excavator had been working. Then the wind ruffling his coat, the blue sky arching above, sharply outlined clouds constantly passing. Birds calling, different ones from those he knew in our back garden, black-headed gulls, peewits, grouse even. All that movement. And over everything, permeating it all, feeding it, the good kind sun. And us, his loved ones who so loved him—that marvellous bond—with him, all enjoying ourselves.

That was true joy, radiant, perfectly innocent.

WEDNESDAY, 11 AUGUST

I know for certain he's been getting into our front garden. He knows he shouldn't. Marianne's afraid he might make a habit of it. We couldn't keep the gate up alongside the house for ever, and our front wall's so low.

I'm only afraid he might be there one day in the driveway when I'm backing the car in. What a thought!

SUNDAY, 15 AUGUST

Had a couple of friends round for lunch. In the afternoon, we all went out for a spin in the car, at least that was the idea. The petrol gauge had been registering empty, but at the first garage there was a bit of a queue, and the youth at the pump was so casual.

"Come on, let's go to the one up Causewayside" I said, "They're cheaper." Blow me! the wretched car runs out of petrol almost at the end of West Savile Terrace. Well, the guests and I had to push it in to the verge, Tam and the girls watching from the pavement. Then we walked to the other garage for a can of the precious juice. Fortunately, they had a spare container. On the way back, the look on that old woman's face as Tam came along, the way she clutched her miniature Yorkshire Terrier to her as he passed.

"Go on, Tam," I murmured, "Give her the works!"

But Marianne was peeved.

"I told you we needed petrol. Why do you always push things too far?"

"Aye, 'push' is the word" I said.

"Oh, you with your silly jokes! You should organise things better. I've told you before."

—Me, organise things? I ask you!

TUESDAY, 17 AUGUST

Caught him at it! Nibbling our parsley in the kitchen garden. No wonder we couldn't get it to grow, and we thought it was the soil. No, as soon as the shoots appeared, he cropped them.

The expression on Tam's face as I rushed out at him, a mixture of mischief and half-guilt (or was it?).

"All right, officer. It's a fair cop."

Then dashed off. Incorrigible, that boy.

WEDNESDAY, 18 AUGUST

Tam loves children, and yet he gives a wide berth to a neighbour's daughter.

This evening, I happened to go out of the back door to empty the tea-leaves by the lilac tree (I know it likes them), when I caught her tormenting Tam.

"Will you stop pulling his tail!" I said.

"I wasn't."

"I saw you with my own eyes."

"I was just holding it."

"Don't tell your lies." I said, "How would *you* like it if someone pulled *your* hair?"

She didn't answer, just walked away, pert little miss. (Tam had stood there, without even deigning to turn his head). And to think we very nearly gave him away.

FRIDAY, 20 AUGUST

Late this afternoon I went to fetch Marianne from the shop. Half-way along busy Morningside Road Tam suddenly flopped down and refused to budge. I had to pick him up and carry him into the doorway of a ladies' clothiers. At first I thought, he's had enough, he always hates the rain, but when I got home with him and he limped into his box and sat there licking his paw, we realised he'd been hurt. In fact his right paw was very swollen, so Catherine bound it up and there he lay, sad-eyed, watching Marianne working in the kitchen. I believe he'd been stung by a bee or a wasp.

Next day he was right as rain.

SATURDAY, 21 AUGUST

This morning weather fine. Out in the front garden, picking off the shoots of the chrysanths and staking them. Tam with me. He especially likes to romp there in the knowledge that it's forbidden territory. When you try to nab him, he has this habit of hiding behind our car— it stands in the wide drive-way—then dashing out at our approach. Even two of us can't catch him.

I'm afraid, when Catherine takes him for a walk she often jumps onto the low wall by our gate with him, instead of going through the gate properly. Marianne's worried this'll only encourage him in his already bad habits.

MONDAY, 30 AUGUST

Who says animals are stupid? Tam is as intelligent as they come and a fine linguist. Better than some of these academic "linguisticians" (horrible word!), I can tell you!

Here are some of the words he understands: "walk" (especially), "toast", "cheese" (how he loves his cheese!), "get in your box" (said reprovingly), "come and sit by the fire", "good boy", "that's naughty" (he doesn't like that at all), "come and have a Polo" (my goodness! doesn't he go wild then), "biscuits", "it's the girls"—that's when Catherine or Elisabeth return from school in the afternoon, and I'm working in the front room, whereupon he gets up and requires to be let out to greet them. He also understands "ball" and "do you want to go in the garden?"

But tea!—"do you want a drink?" or "do you want some tea?"— the phrases have long been music to his ears. Whenever we brew up at various times of the day we give him his share. At 9 pm we make ourselves a pot to accompany the news on television—well, you need something to fortify you, with the things you see! He knows the beverage is in the offing, and he'll then "get in his box", which he knows means being "a good boy" and sit upright, listening to the kettle whistle, watching my every move as I heat the pot, take down the tea-caddy, put in three teaspoonfuls, then pour the boiling water in. He doesn't like his tea hot, as we have it, but lukewarm, and he's partial to plenty of milk and no sugar. Tea-bags are perfectly in order.

While I'm on the subject of food and drink, I must tell you he has a sweet tooth. Fruit drops, mints, assorted balls—hard sweets of any kind—he doesn't suck but crunches them, loudly. He has difficulty with toffees, his teeth not being fashioned for soft stretchy caramel, and has to spit the mass out a couple of times before he can finally get it down. Nor does he find Rowntree's Clear Gums easy. For some reason—perhaps it's the bright colours—he treats them like little toys or flies. He'll sit there in his sphinx position, ready to play, and push the gum a little across the carpet (great fun if it happens to roll!), teasing you with it for quite a while before he attempts to eat it. He's also partial to a chunk of ice.

I'm afraid he still ransacks the wastepaper baskets if left on the floor. We've now got into the habit of placing them on the sideboard or bookcase. Whenever the girls and I are eating sweets, he'll immediately go for any of our discarded wrappers and chew them, then come and sit nearby, upright, on the cadge, willing you soundlessly to give him some. He'll also ransack the wastepaper baskets for apple-cores, banana-skins and suchlike. Anything going, in fact—he's not choosy.

70

SUNDAY, 5 SEPTEMBER

We've been meaning for ages to go rose-hip picking over Blackford Hill to make jelly. This afternoon we went, just Marianne and I, plus Tam of course.

We'd left it rather late, but in the end, we did find a couple of bushes up a steep bank the other side of Corbie's Craig, by Blackford Quarry. Tam's so active we were obliged to tie him by his lead to a nearby bush, while we picked the hips, putting them into plastic bags— a bit on the mushy side, I noticed.

So there he sits in the sun on an uncomfortable perch high up the slope amongst scree, watching us sadly, looking as if he'd like to help but not knowing quite how. I had to interrupt my picking to go across and stroke him.

THURSDAY, 9 SEPTEMBER

Marianne's mother and Otto, her cousin, have come to stay with us.

I don't know how we got onto the subject, but last night, Otto and I were talking about this propensity of Tam's of rolling in horse-manure or sheep-droppings. Otto thinks it's an ancient canine instinct with a sensible reason behind it. By overlaying itself with the scent of other animals, the dog can put any potential pursuer off.

—He certainly put us off!

FRIDAY, 10 SEPTEMBER

There's nothing Otto likes more than taking Tam for a walk. Tam knows the exact times of day when there's one in the offing and comes and stands or sits by him, ready. They're inseparable; I'm getting quite jealous.

For rainy weather—we've had quite a lot lately—Marianne's made Tam a waistcoat of green and red checked flannel with cloth straps that go underneath ("belly bands" I call them) which button up. He wears it under silent protest, as if to say "What's the point in going out anyway if it's raining?"

When you attach his lead to his collar, he'll get on his back, presenting his neck and yet growl and snap at you, but not seriously. He never does this when you take his lead off after or during a walk so he can have a run. He just stands there, docile. It's perfectly understandable, I suppose: liberation is always easier than capture.

But in the open—I noticed especially today, when I saw him with Otto—seen from a distance, he's really quite a small dog, lean and sharp.

FRIDAY, 10 SEPTEMBER

Sometimes at the prospect of a walk or on welcoming one of us home he'll be so excited that his sexual urge is roused, and you'll see his small penis erect, bright red against the black of his coat for a moment, before it pops in again. He doesn't play with his penis, as a cat will. None of the languid voluptuousness I've observed in the cat I kept as a boy.

That bright intensity of his, all his own. If he wants something, he wants it hard, and yet you can substitute one bait for another and decoy him. You can, for all his love of a chase, get him to come in, simply by saying "Come and have a Polo", or "come and get a biscuit". Occasionally he may pause, but only for a moment.

THURSDAY, 16 SEPTEMBER

Yesterday afternoon no classes. Went kiting with Catherine and Otto on Blackford Hill. Naturally Tam was with us. One of those fresh brighty blowy late-summer days, still some warmth in the sun.

I made the kite myself, as I'd promised Catherine, of canes, brown paper and string, sticking it together with a paste of flour and water. Not being the practical kind, I was dead proud of it—far better than those fabricated Japanese models! And like a poem, it came to life. It flew, it flew!

How excited Tam was, once we'd released him up there! It was so windy on the summit that all four yards of tail, with a rag tied at the bottom, fluttered wildly as the kite rose. Like a water-snake it suddenly streaked down into an expanse of waving grass, whereupon Tam dashed across to try and get in amongst it. We'd rescue the kite, send it up, and then he'd stare at the length of string arching up. Oh! to get entangled in that string, those tails, to pull this way and that, to get your teeth into it, and tug! How he relished the excitement of the moment!—"Brio", musicians call it, and after all, isn't every good piece of music made up of a series of miraculous momentary inspirations, controlled spontaneity?

On the way down we passed a slide that children had made. A few lads, sitting on big pieces of cardboard—Kellogg's Cornflake boxes and suchlike—came whizzing down, laughing. The grass was so dry that the leather soles of your shoes shone, indeed the surface was as slippery as the black glass of a schoolyard slide.

Tam launches into the fray, chasing one poor kid as he slides downhill, barking and snapping away at the cardboard.

"Don't be scared!" I shout, "He won't attack you. It's the cardboard he's after."

Finally he wrenches it out, causing the lad to tumble downhill, whereupon he assumes his sheep-dog posture, daring us to come and

72

get it. Thank goodness, the lad's all right and we've a few Polos on us!
What a handful! Sometimes I wonder what will become of him.

THURSDAY, 30 SEPTEMBER

The evenings are now beginning to draw in. Last night we brought
Sam's box into the cloakroom—it gets too cold in the porch once the
sun goes down.

Sam makes his demands too. Whenever anyone opens the pantry
door, it's not long before he starts rattling at the wire mesh on the
front of his cage for a carrot or his greens. He nearly always rattles the
same spot in the mesh—bottom left—and his little teeth can't half tug
and wrench! It's the same in the morning, whereas now Tam lies quiet.
Whenever Sam's taken out and given the run of our living-room, he'll
usually make for a favourite spot under the armchair by the fire
(usually leaving a present of droppings for Tam). But if the door is left
open, he'll almost invariably scuttle across and out across the hall to
his cage in the cloakroom, and there he'll sit, waiting to be readmitted,
frightened of too much freedom. You should see his caramel-coloured
fat rump anxiously humping it over the board and in.

Sam's slowing down, though he hasn't lost any of his appetite; he
sleeps more and likes his comforts. He also drags one leg a little from
an accident he had some time ago. In a word he's beginning to age,
whereas Tam's now come into his own. Sam's already lived four or
five years and it's not been a bad life so far. Well, we'll do our best
to ensure he enjoys a good old age.

Tonight Elisabeth had him on her lap in front of the fire and was
stroking him. Tam lying there at her feet, quite content. Who would
have thought it possible?

WEDNESDAY, 6 OCTOBER

All this rabies scare in the news. Well, I'm all for the strictest
quarantine. I'll never forget that dog I saw in a country road near
Nuremberg in 1959 in a rabies-ridden area. It looked like a cross
between an alsation and an Irish wolfhound, it was so large. It was
clear it had the disease, standing there in the middle of the road, stock
still in the hot sun, its mouth slavering, its eyes blood-shot, staring.
You could feel the menace coming from it, for all the protection of the
car. Evil personified, poisonous, baleful. We reversed and reported the
case to the nearest police station.

From the start we've been punctilious over hygiene. We never let
Tam lick the girl's faces. If Catherine—for instance—happened to kiss

him, she was told off and made to go and wash. If any of us handle him before a meal, we always wash our hands. You can't be too careful.

When my mother-in-law stayed with us I noticed how over-fastidious she was, how she always stroked him with distaste, but in time, as she got fond of him, she became less squeamish. I've noticed Marianne and I both react the same way to dogs and to Tam in particular. I suppose it's a matter of balance—like most things.

THURSDAY, 7 OCTOBER

Tam's a clean dog, as I say, but sometimes in the mornings he'll have sleep in his eyes, especially if he has a bit of a cold. Then he doesn't seem to bother about getting it out. We wipe him clean with a paper handkerchief, and he seems grateful for our attentions.

I remember how as a little puppy he used to dribble onto our hall carpet, such was his gladness to see one of us first thing in the morning, before allowing himself to be thrust out of the back door!

SUNDAY, 10 OCTOBER

Once Tam's finished his business in the back garden and is ready to come in, he'll simply sit quite still on the back doorstep. Only if the weather is particularly bad, like today—rain and high winds—will he cry gently for admittance.

WEDNESDAY, 20 OCTOBER

He can stand on his hind legs for four or five seconds at a time and prance and twist in the air as well as any circus dog. He performs best when he's after something, as footballers rise highest when they're trying to beat their opponents in the air, or cyclists ride fastest when chasing a pace-maker.

SUNDAY, 24 OCTOBER

Though he doesn't snore, he'll murmur in his sleep, quick soft grunts through his nose, rather like the sounds made by old people as they loll forward, dropping off before a television set.

Marianne nudged me in bed last night.

"Listen, Derek, can you hear? He's at it again."

He'd be lying there, curled at the foot of the stairs, waiting for us, warming that patch of carpet.

I thought of the deep carrying murmur of my parents' voices coming from their bedroom when I was a boy, soothing me as I lay there in Liverpool years ago.

WEDNESDAY, 3 NOVEMBER

Sometimes when he's been cooped up at home, I'll run with him pell-mell along Cluny Gardens, giving him his head for the length of a few houses (on the lead of course). After fifty yards or so I'm out of breath; he's still warming up.

When he knows we're going up to the allotments, he races up Midmar Avenue like a whippet. He knows he'll soon be off his lead.

Then I think, I shouldn't really be exciting him like this. What he needs is tranquillizers. They do have them for dogs, I believe.

THURSDAY, 4 NOVEMBER

When we go past shops I have to watch out for the boxes on display outside, or those dark green sacks of wastepaper for the refuse collector. He's liable to pee on them unless checked. He pulls from this side to the other, criss-crossing in front of me, now sniffing the fish-shops and butchers' shops, now snaffling the odd chip or gobbling a potato skin in the doorway of Mr Chukityleaf's Baked Potato Shop, now dragging me over to a crate of milk-bottles by the kerb. I'm reminded of Elisabeth as a toddler on the Isle of Wight years ago and how she leaned at an angle of 45°, as we walked along the sloping shore, with me holding her hand; she was so drawn to the sea.

When Tam and I stand at the lights, waiting for the green man to appear, "the boy", just to show how well-behaved he can be when he tries, will sit nicely at the kerb, then trot demurely across, glancing back at me, as if to say "Good, eh?"

The trouble is, he's not consistent.

FRIDAY, 5 NOVEMBER

I've just been watching him from the kitchen through our hatch. He comes into the living-room, eyes a rolled-up ball of my grey socks on the cabinet. First he glances about, then gets up on his hind legs, and, tempted, cranes his head forward only to falter at the last minute, somehow able to quell the urge, and drop back sadly to the floor then trail off, casting a longing look behind.

Socks or hankies left draped over the radiator are fair game. It's up to us to put them elsewhere or keep him out of the room. We both know that. He's established his right to them.

MONDAY, 8 NOVEMBER

When I walk him down Comiston Road he gets all worked up. It's the memory of that schoolyard of kids stored in his brain. And if, as tonight, school is already out, you can sense his disappointment.

FRIDAY, 12 NOVEMBER

Late afternoon. I take up my favourite position in the front room for a quiet read. Catherine's just brought in a tray of tea and home-made scones, warmed under the grill, with melted butter and straw-berry-jam. Having perused the *Times,* I turn to *Private Eye.*

All of a sudden I hear Elisabeth shout *"TAM!"*—He's just snatched something off one of the girls and shot under the sideboard, his paws scratching the floor-boards as he whizzes under-cover. The daft thing still thinks he's safe under there. I suppose he always will.

SATURDAY, 13 NOVEMBER

Tam back to his evening viewing, like the rest of us. "Match of the Day"—it's still his favourite. He takes a grandstand seat, curled up on the pouffé in front of the fire. I'm afraid it's now become too small for him, with the result that one of his legs, not to mention his bushy tail, lies flopped over the side.

He takes a lively enough interest, as it is, in the game, but let any sheep appear on the screen, and in a flash, he sharpens. Up he shoots to face the set and bark at it, at *them,* those silly creatures that always need shepherding. Intently he watches their every move, and if they wander to the right and off the screen he must think they've gone into our garden, for he jumps up at the window, rests his forepaws on the window-ledge and stares out into the dark. He remains there for ten or twenty seconds, agog, then thoroughly frustrated, he moves restlessly about the room for awhile (strange, he doesn't ask to be let out), then finally relaxes and resumes his former position on the pouffé. He acts the same way whenever he sees other animals on the television or hears a dog barking in a neighbour's house or garden, though he's not so intense on these occasions.

MONDAY, 15 NOVEMBER

I wonder if Catherine's strict enough with him. She lays him on his back, for instance, then places him on her lap—he hates that—and tickles his tummy. He'll even growl. Is it not bad for his spine? After all, he's not just a toy, nor even just a pet, he's one of the family.

WEDNESDAY, 1 DECEMBER

Let's face it, he's not always as obedient as he should be. When he's off his lead, he'll lark about on the pavement or in the gutter, or even go into the road. Then, if you try to put his lead back on, sometimes he'll hop away and trot ahead a few yards or lurk behind, teasing. Usually he's docile, depending on his mood. We've taken him along roads often enough, and the girls, Elisabeth especially, have really tried hard to train him. You don't mind a bit of lee-way in a quiet street, but where *is* safe these days?

If we take him past Blackford Pond and up the hill by the Observatory, where there are always a number of other dogs, we get him to come to heel—at least that's the theory—by arming ourselves with a packet of Polos and biscuits. But now even *they* don't always work, if he sees another dog he really likes. Still it doesn't matter so much up there.

Once tuned into his wavelength, how amazingly rich a walk can be! The world is at your feet, bursting to give utterance, there for the taking. It's no wonder he won't be bound.

THURSDAY, 2 DECEMBER

Late afternoon, into town in the car with Catherine to fetch Marianne from work. She finishes at 5.30. By the time we're passing the Meadow Bar along Buccleuch Street it's 5.25, already dark and the height of the rush-hour. There's a long queue of cars standing in the opposite direction, held up by the lights at the corner of the Meadows. It's raining, headlamps dazzle, rear-lights glow red. Suddenly a woman with a couple of kids steps out from behind a car. My heart gives a jump, I brake hard. The woman and her children (one held by the hand, the other walking free) cross. They don't even turn a hair.

Later I said to Marianne

"I must always give myself time. It's fatal to drive against the clock."

MONDAY, 6 DECEMBER

You should see the two of them there in the kitchen, Sam sitting contentedly, munching a piece of apple, while Tam roots about, not angry or jealous, waiting patiently for Sam to leave him his present. Tam even allows the guinea-pig a share of his milk, though he stays

77

away while the latter partakes. None of us have ever seen the pair of them scrapping, and if they'd fought behind our backs, it would have shown. After Sam's been around, however, Tam carefully sniffs the whole area.

TUESDAY, 22 DECEMBER

Of late—and this is disturbing—he's started roaming. We've only caught him at it a couple of times, but that's enough.

Last night a colleague of mine called round; we were going to the Hermitage Bar for a drink. When I opened the door he stood there, holding "the boy" by his collar. He'd discovered him on the other side of the road. We ordered Tam into his box. But what can you do?

Marianne mentioned this propensity of Tam's to a colleague at work today, who recalled a dog with the self-same sheepdog wildness in him.

"I'm afraid" she said, "the older he grew, the wilder he got. What's bred in the bone. . . . He took to leaving the house and roaming for three or four days at a time. He always came back though, but where he got to, I never found out. Certainly none of the neighbours could tell us. In the end we had to give him away. We were fortunate though, we found a farmer willing to take him."

WEDNESDAY, 23 DECEMBER

This morning Catherine and I went to Dofo's along Morningside Road to buy Tam a Christmas present. Of course he must go and cock his leg up against the corner of the counter and give it a sprinkling! Many a dog must have done it in its time and the scent got him going. Anyway the girl didn't seem to mind.

Catherine chose two presents, the first an appalling dark-grey turd-like object with a roughish surface. Edible, so we were told. It reminds me of what used to be sold under the name of "Dirty Fido" in "The Wizard's Den" in Liverpool. What a splendid place that was! The second was a dog-biscuit, shaped like a bone, and tightly enclosed in cellophane. Tam immediately knew they were for him. He doesn't miss much, that boy.

Catherine let him carry the bone home in his mouth. A rare sight—we've never trusted him with a rolled-up newspaper or suchlike.

"What daft presents!" says Marianne, when we get back, "honestly, have you nothing better to do with your money?"

"I don't agree." I say, "I like a child with a bit of imagination."

"Well, she's got that all right. Just like her Dad."

"I take that as a compliment. Come on, what's for dinner?"

FRIDAY, 24 DECEMBER

But he does like his sweets. Not the "Good Boy" variety—awful sickly white chocolatey lozenges that they are, only fit for middle-aged pekinese and poodles! No, *real* sweets, the sort human beings eat.

What kinds? Well, apart from the ones I've mentioned, chocolate of any kind—Cadbury's Bourneville, plain or dairy milk, "Galaxy", "Aero", plain or mint flavour, Cadbury's Fruit and Nut, and chocolates of course. Orkney fudge is also a favourite, though he finds it hard to chew.

He'll eat a segment of orange, though he has a job coping with the stringy flesh. But doesn't he relish the juice!

These last few evenings he's been sitting at our feet by the fire, waiting to be thrown his share of nuts. He loves them all, chestnuts, shoe-nuts (brazils), walnuts, pea-nuts (Marianne's been roasting them on baking trays in the oven and salting them). We must have thrown him scores and still he comes back for more. The noise he makes, as he cracks them between his beautiful white teeth, his jaws snapping like a live pair of nut-crackers!

SUNDAY, 26 DECEMBER

Took Tam for a walk in the afternoon. Felt so bloated from all the food and drink and sitting about. Again I noticed how he gives car-exhausts a wide berth, whenever we pass them in drive-ways. He must have got a whiff sometime or other.

Again he must go and do his business right against the gate of the Church on the corner. He's also partial to doing it on the pebbles and grit in the open drive-ways of posh houses. Does he resent the Scottish protestant-capitalist-nexus?

When he's off his leash and does his business out in the open, on Blackford Hill, say, or on the bank by the allotments along Midmar Drive, then, once it's done, he'll turn his back on you and kick up the soil and grass with rapid vigorous backward scrapes of his back paws. I believe he's trying to cover his tracks.

MONDAY, 27 DECEMBER

Catherine has this habit of attaching a long elastic band to a piece of material and dangling it over the banisters. Every time Tam snaps at it, she pulls it up. It's a wonder he doesn't get really angry with her. Catherine and I sometimes play "piggy in the middle", with him as "piggy". Goodness me, how he gets carried away! He may be a bit on the reckless side, but I'll say this for him, there's never a trace of mumpishness about him. He can growl, but not often, only to establish and maintain his rights, and they're usually reasonable, if you consider them carefully enough.

—"Makes a lively contribution", as we used to write when I was a schoolmaster, on the reports of those pests you sometimes get.

TUESDAY, 28 DECEMBER

This morning, over Blackford Hill with Tam and the girls, and down into the Dell, across the bridge (no fear now on the part of "the boy"), over the Braid Burn, along the path by the cows (Tam barking through the railings), and up across the golf-course. Bracing winter weather, Tam's coat ruffling in the wind.

Over Blackford Hill Catherine starts teasing him. When he went dashing on ahead, she whispered to Elisabeth and me.

"Quick! hide behind this bramble-bush, just you watch his reaction when he sees we're gone."

And sure enough, before long, "the boy" stops in his tracks, glances round, and missing us, pauses, clearly worried; finally he scampers back in search of us. At his approach we all jumped out with a laugh, and he was all over us, dear Tam!, jumping up, trying to lick our faces, before we could stop him. What a relief to find we hadn't disappeared after all!

"It's all right, Tam" said Elisabeth, making a fuss of him, "Don't worry, we'll always be here for you. You'll be safe, quite safe."

WEDNESDAY, 29 DECEMBER

This morning, cold clear weather. Took Tam for a walk. As we were walking along Cluny Gardens, all of a sudden, he started back in fear, dug his heels in, and refused to budge. The only cause I could discover was a big yellow skip standing in the road. I pulled him past it while he kept as close as possible to the garden fence. It was exactly the same on the way back.

Anything out of the ordinary can disturb him. I've often noticed how he gives dustbins a wide berth. He also seems puzzled when I smoke my pipe. There must be a connection somewhere.

Certainly he seems to suffer intense yet inexplicable fears. I've seen him start in his sleep as if in the throes of a nightmare.

*   *   *   *   *

Those eyes of his, flashing, now brown, now blue, now grey. The world seems to go straight into them, straight into his eager spirit.

THURSDAY, 30 DECEMBER

A long-cherished ambition of Tam's achieved at last!

I spent yesterday afternoon and early evening interpreting for an Edinburgh firm who were negotiating the take-over of a German firm. (Nice to see it that way round for once). The German business-manager went on to spend the rest of the evening with us at home. After the meal, Herr S., Marianne and I sat in the front room sipping whisky and talking into the night, with Tam snoozing at our feet in front of the fire.

It was about 1.30 am before we drove Herr S. back to his hotel, The Post House, by Edinburgh Zoo. We took Tam along as a treat. He sat there in the back, good as gold, taking everything in.

When we arrived at the hotel, however, we had a job restraining "the boy". He can shoot off in a flash, if you don't watch out, which is just what he did. Fortunately, such was the strangeness of the place, he stopped a few yards away, indecisive. Marianne grabbed him, plonked him on the back seat, and locked the door.

After saying goodbye to our guest the situation was different. On the way out Marianne had sat with Tam on the back seat with us two men at the front; now on the return journey, Marianne sat with me in front Tam, immediately sizing up the situation, refused to stay at the back, nor would he crouch or lie on the floor at Marianne's feet. He was determined to see everything—and this time up front. He was quite adamant. Well, after a few squirms and fumbles, Marianne got him to sit quiet on her knee.

Was he pleased! A point made, a new right established. He's just like the Russians in this—and not only them.

FRIDAY, 31 DECEMBER

He's at it again, sitting there upright, intent, by my table in the front room:

"Please, master" he's saying, "Please take me for a walk. I can't stand being cooped up here any longer. How can you sit there? Come on, let's go. Now. Right now!"

I'm finding it harder and harder to resist, till of late I've been going for walks two or three times a day, to grant him this pleasure, no, not mere pleasure, his heart's desire. He *must* roam.

What's he after? Freedom? But who can attain it as absolutely as he needs it? I'm only a sedentary townsman after all. I can't get my work done with him impelling me like this. Ah, Tam, if only you knew! Don't ask for too much.

There's something frantic about it. Who's to blame? It's crazy, he's pushing me too much. I must be firmer with him, after all I *am* his master.

PART TWO

1977

TUESDAY, 4 JANUARY

Yesterday afternoon Catherine and I went for a walk with Tam, just a short walk so as to get back in time for "Poppy", a film on the television, starring the great W. C. Fields.

Before we went out I rang up the Lothian Water Board because I'd seen a burst tap in a field at the top of Midmar Drive, with water gushing out all over the place. The man at the other end of the line promised to send someone over to see to it.

We went up Midmar Avenue, and as soon as we reached the allotments, we let Tam off his leash. Away he streaked, then he dawdled, letting us get ahead before rushing past us. So we proceeded along the path past the allotments up Midmar Drive to the fields at the top. There Catherine climbed over the fence, while Tam flattened himself under, to go and see the water-trough at close quarters.

All around were frozen lumps of ice where the escaped water had bounced. While Catherine crunched them underfoot, Tam stood clear, doubtless concerned about the pads of his feet. Meanwhile a tramp was approaching from the copse in the adjoining sheep-field. Middle-aged, with a ruddy complexion, wild eyes, and with great bunches of grey hair protruding from under an old green beret, he presented a frightening figure, as he wheeled his bike through the grass. He reached a gap in the fence, lowered his bike to the ground and started to pull off laths from the fence.

We turned away and resumed our walk along Hermitage Drive past the large quiet expensive houses. Only the occasional car, hardly anyone about, everything safe. Tam was off his lead and docile enough.

We turned right into Braid Road, Tam crossing at my bidding, then right again into Braid Crescent. Here he was a bit naughty and wouldn't come round the corner until I went back and insisted, and then he refused to stay on the pavement.

Two lads were playing cricket on the pavement, using a lamp-post for wickets. By then it was beginning to grow dark and a slight grey mist hung in the air. All was quiet, the occasional light going on here and there in the houses.

We turned left down Hermitage Gardens, then right into Corrennie Drive where the occasional occupant, generally elderly, could be seen, reading or writing by the light of a lamp near a window. We then turned into Braid Avenue, having got Tam back on to his lead, crossed the road, and turned right into Cluny Drive, another quiet road of substantial houses, properties well kept up, eminently respectable.

We turned into Midmar Avenue, with Tam still on his lead. The traffic was, as usual, busy along Cluny Gardens when we finally crossed. It was getting on for four o'clock by now and already quite dark. I was looking forward to the film. We walked towards our gate, only fifty yards to go.

At the bus-stop, Catherine slipped Tam off his lead. For some time he'd been accustomed to being released a few yards before our gate, when he would trot along the pavement close to the garden-walls and enter our gate, if it was open, or wait patiently, if it was shut. This time, however, there was a group of people over the other side of the road by the entrance to Braid Tennis Club, and they had a dog with them. Tam spotted it. Catherine shouted "Stay!", but he ignored her and darted straight out into the path of a fast car. It hit him head on and flung him sideways into the gutter from where he lurched, yelping, through the gate into the house.

The driver braked, and stopped on the other side of the road. He came over to our gate, apologizing, but you couldn't really blame him. Thinking the dog must be all right, he apologized again, crossed the road to his car and drove off.

Marianne and Elisabeth, hearing the screech of brakes, had dashed out of the house. As we went back inside I kept on accusing Catherine of carelessness.

Tam must have made straight for the sideboard, for there he lay, under the right hand side. I fetched his battered cardboard-box out of the kitchen, placed it by the fire in the living-room and, having lifted him out carefully from his lair, laid him in the box and wrapped him in a blanket.

He lay on his side, his trembling flanks moving the blanket slightly. I stroked him, his hair all wet with sweat and dirty from the road. Occasionally I could feel a shiver go through him. There was no sign of injury, not a fleck of blood. I kept on stroking him, hoping against hope he was all right. Outside in the hall, Marianne was searching frenziedly through the yellow pages of the telephone directory for a vet. Finally she dictated a message to an answering machine, asking the vet to come immediately.

Elisabeth crouched beside me. Tam was now clearly in a bad way. The upsurge of hope I'd felt when he managed to struggle indoors was ebbing away. I could hardly feel his heart beat. He gasped for air twice, each gasp followed by a sigh, then his tongue lolled from his mouth. I looked at his eyes, they were dead. Elisabeth felt his heart, it was quite still.

O God, it was a terrible moment!

Catherine kept on crying "Oh why? Oh why?" Marianne came in, looked down at him and said "It's all over. You'd better ring the vet and tell him there's no need to come."

Elisabeth couldn't settle, she said she must go and see one of her friends. She had to get out at all costs. As she left the house I called "Don't be late coming back!" It was still only 4.30, everything had happened in less than half an hour.

When we examined Tam there were no signs of broken bones or lacerations. He might have broken his neck, but I'm no expert. Certainly the neck and brisket were all floppy. Elisabeth thought the shock was simply too much for his heart.

We couldn't leave him there, so Catherine and I decided to bury him in the garden. Marianne started giving the house a good going-over in order to relieve her feelings. Catherine took Tam and carried him down the garden-path, still crying, down to the apple-trees at the bottom.

It was dark and chilly by now. I pulled on a thick pullover and joined Catherine down by the shed. I took out a fork and spade. I was shivering with cold when I started to dig.

We dug the hole under the bottom apple-tree. It wasn't easy, since the ground was frozen. I dug and dug, with Catherine helping me as best she could. We had to enlarge the hole a few times. Tam, laid out, was larger than I thought, and I didn't want to harm his forelegs or hocks. We then put my old gardening pullover under him— I didn't want him to rest on the bare soil. We laid him flat on his side in the shallow grave and covered him with one of Catherine's old pullovers he'd been fond of playing with.

The patch was full of bluebell bulbs which were now scattered all over the place. We gave him a parting kiss, "Poor Tam, we do love you", then covered him up and I rammed a slate into the soil above his head as a memorial, thumping it in with the flat of my spade. Then we two bowed our heads and I said a prayer, thanking God for the privilege of having Tam in our midst and thanking him for giving us all so much joy—for joy it was in the exact sense of the word, pure, perfectly innocent—and we wished him a quiet rest. Finally I put away the tools, locked the shed, and we returned to the house. Catherine had been helping the whole time. I was relieved that she was keeping herself busy.

*   *   *

Marianne, Catherine and I were completely at a loss how to spend the evening. Such a sense of chaos. I especially didn't want Catherine to sit and brood, so I got her to read aloud a couple of stories she'd written some time ago and to finish one she'd started.

I sat by the fire in our living-room, watched her writing. It was so quiet I could hear her pen scratching. It was all I could do, apart from ringing up Elisabeth's friend to see if she was all right, and could she make her own way back.

Then Catherine, having asked if we were hungry, made some toasted cheese, fetching a glass of red wine for me, and a small glass of cider for herself. To follow, we ate a little chocolate cake she'd baked earlier during the day—she loves cooking. (Marianne wasn't hungry).

We three stayed close together in the living-room. Elisabeth came back about 9 o'clock. She was very quiet, which is not like here. I decided to bath Catherine, a thing I haven't done for years. I went upstairs, ran a hot bath for her, washed her all over, and dried her carefully. Then I washed and dried her long hair. Meanwhile Marianne was watching the news on the television; she couldn't settle to anything else.

I went up and sat with Catherine in bed and read the captions to the pictures in her Oxford Junior Encyclopaedia, a new Christmas present, up to the end of the letter "C", after which I read her the beautiful section on "Childbirth". (The volume in which it is contained is entitled "Home and Health"). I then read to myself the section on "Conversation", sitting up against the headboard, with Catherine lying beside me. I began to feel weary. By then it was 9.30.

I went downstairs and joined Marianne, then shortly after returned upstairs to give myself a good bath. I'd asked Marianne for a cup of hot chocolate and she had it ready when I finished. When I returned downstairs, the girls were watching television, Catherine in her pyjamas and dressing gown, but I said, no, I didn't think it was appropriate, and switched the set off. The girls went off to bed.

Once they'd settled I went upstairs to them and we said our prayers, including a special one for Tam and we thought about him for a moment. I then tucked them in, gave them a kiss and, sitting on the bed, tried to say a few words of consolation.

Not long after ten o'clock Marianne and I were in bed ourselves.

*   *   *

Troubled night. Two cruel dreams.

The first was of receiving a telephone-call from the departmental secretary at the University to say I'd be so glad to learn Tam had been found and was perfectly all right. The relief I felt! In a great wave it flooded over me, only to wake up and realize afresh the horror of his death. The experience was the exact opposite of a nightmare.

The second was of standing in an antique shop, talking cordially to an old friend of mine. I was a kind of customer, he the proprietor. While we talked as one friend to another, I noticed standing outside his window, which was rather empty and neglected, two close relatives of his who'd lost a son some years ago in a tragic accident. They were making signs, asking if they might enter, not imperiously or impatiently, but quietly, courteously. My friend went over and asked them into his shop to talk to me. Their presence promised relief, a soothing of my pain. Then I woke up once more to reality.

WEDNESDAY, 5 JANUARY

We all got up at half-past eight yesterday morning, with no Tam to greet us at the bottom of the stairs. Later Marianne said to me "I had to put the washing out all by myself."

I just got up instinctively from my table in the front room to move the tray of tea-things that Catherine had brought in and put on the couch. As I was walking across I checked myself, "There's no need to put it on top of the piano any more."

THURSDAY, 6 JANUARY

As I lay in bed last night Tam kept on coming into my mind, granting me no peace.

The pang I felt this morning at the kitchen-sink when I found a piece of toast left over in the bread-basket. He'd automatically have got it— he'd have been in and out of my legs there. I broke it up, opened the window and threw the bits out to the birds.

Unable to settle, I went upstairs where Marianne was busy hoovering the landing. (Whenever she's under strain, she works all the harder). I sat down on the landing, leaning against the wall. She stopped hoovering, and we talked for a while about Tam. Everything was tangled, like the wire of the vacuum cleaner which has always been too long.

I remember how Elisabeth, when she was a small girl, would plant herself on my lap after breakfast—of all times!—hand me her doll, Angela, and say in her childish peremptory manner "Talk about Angela!", and I'd be obliged to invent a story about her doll and her, weaving my daughter into language and the human experience it enmeshes, through her feelings for her doll.

I went downstairs and asked Elisabeth if she'd like to go for a walk, but she didn't, not just the two of us.

I've even returned to playing the piano after a respite of several years. We stick together, the four of us, as much as possible. Everything's so bitty at the moment. Marianne went back to work. Let's hope it'll help.

FRIDAY, 7 JANUARY

Got up at 7.30 am, after lying awake for a while. Again two dreams about Tam.

In the first I was in the suburb of a large town, just like Liverpool, standing in a wide road on a modern council estate, the landscape of my boyhood. There were shops along the avenue, built well back and separated from the road by a wide pavement. Not many people about, everything quietish, normal. Suddenly there's action! A man has stolen something from one of the shops, he dashes out, crosses the pavement, gets onto a motorbike and kicks the starter. Now he's speeding towards me, straight at me, but strangely, not a sound is coming from him, nor do I feel any sense of danger at his approach. There's simply no question of my being run over. I feel such buoyancy in myself, I can tackle him single-handed, this thief, and take back whatever he's stolen.

I woke up and again the horror of Tam's death came over me. I dropped off and dreamt again. It was extremely vivid and much more unpleasant this time.

Marianne and I were at a party given by a friend of ours, a successful academic. We were sitting comfortably in the elegantly appointed sitting-room of his modern flat on thickly padded armchairs, drinking and talking. Everything was going fine, the whole company enjoying themselves, well-disposed towards one another. Suddenly I had such toothache. I was aware I'd had a tooth extracted recently, a large molar half-way along the lower left jaw. Inside the great tender cavity a very large clot had formed. It bulged slightly, and I had to probe it with my tongue. How round it was! Ah!, suddenly it came away. What a spongy, squashy mass, and it was beginning to disintegrate in my mouth. Ugh!, that rust taste of blood. How could I possibly contain all that sloppy mass, all that blood in my mouth?— *and* in front of all these people talking away, smiling, drinking, laughing unconcerned! Somehow I must get out, and with a minimum of fuss, at all costs get to the bathroom. By now I'm bleeding profusely, I can feel the blood welling up inside, making me hold my lips tight, my mouth's so full. How awful to have a trickle, however thin, slip down my chin in front of all these people! How on earth can I smile now, keep up appearances! Ah! thank goodness!, at last I'm out in the corridor. I go along, treading the thick pile carpet—everything about the place is new and glossy—musn't make a mess—how long the corridor is! and there, through the open kitchen door I see my host, busy making coffee. He smiles, greets me. How can I possibly respond? "I only hope he won't be offended", I think through all the dull ache in my jaw, and my face like a football-trainer's orange coloured rubber spongebag full of blood. At last I'm in the bathroom. I feel so bad, but ah! at last I can let these clots out and all that blood flow freely into the sink, that dull ache streaming. Both taps are full on, sluicing it away. Will it ever end?

SATURDAY, 8 JANUARY

Tam's tongue lolling out of his mouth. The image haunts me. Bulging, purplish, grainy, like a huge parrot's tongue, only slopped out. Ugly.

Marianne's mother rang up from Germany this evening. Marianne told her all about Tam. Her mother called him "ein treuer Kerl", "a staunch fellow"—that just about sums him up.

SUNDAY, 9 JANUARY

This evening Marianne, the girls and I watched a film on television about crocodiles. One tore a deer to bits under water with its innumerable needle-fine teeth, then a dog. The way it sank those teeth into the pale flesh, hanging and swaying from the carcase, in the water, then, still attached, it suddenly jerked itself over, thus ripping the flesh away. That intentness, whippiness, a creature glorying in what it was made to do. The process would go on until all the flesh was off.

* * *

My sister used to have this habit of saying things like "This time next Monday I'll be sitting on the train going to London," or "This time in a fortnight we'll be on the beach at Rhyl." Only with her it was looking forward to things, whereas I keep on dwelling on that ghastly moment of impact. If only he hadn't been slipped off his lead. Why didn't I think? He was entrusted to us, we were supposed to be looking after him.

"In future I'll enjoy the present more" I say to myself.—Daft thoughts.

MONDAY, 10 JANUARY

Spring term starts today.

This awful sense of guilt. In spasms, no real let-up. Like standing in a London tube station when you suddenly feel an icy rush of bad underground air, and you can't avoid it.

I received a letter this morning from my uncle in North Wales, saying his two dogs had died, aged 13 and 14—of old age.

Every time I see someone walking his dog I think, he's looking after it properly. Not like me.

THURSDAY, 13 JANUARY

These great "long vehicles" packed full of sheep and cows—two tiers of them—from the Borders, going to the slaughterhouse, that come past our house every week as regular as clockwork. I remember the calf I saw slaughtered in Saarburg, Marianne's home town, years ago. Even when its head had been severed from its trunk, now lying there flat out, the hoofs continued clattering on the wet tiled floor.

Pathetic, how Tam made for under the sideboard, as if there's ever anywhere safe: "The past has already gone, the future has not yet arrived and the present has no duration" (St Augustine).

FRIDAY, 14 JANUARY

Spoke to the postman this morning about Tam's death. He'd been missing him (I have to tell everyone, I'm just like my mother in this). He said "If I had a place like yours, a proper house with a garden, not a poky little flat, I'd keep a dog. What a shame, though! He was always so friendly."

He agreed ours was a dangerous road. But where isn't nowadays?

SUNDAY, 16 JANUARY

As we were getting up this morning Catherine said to me "Come and have a look at this".

She took out from under her bed her collection—Tam's feeding bowl, his three leads, his collar with his name and address-plate hanging on it, his blue superball, even the little red plastic Watney's barrel.

Elisabeth's now collected all the snaps she could find of him and put them in an album which she keeps in a drawer in her bedroom. On the corner of a photograph of her college friends that stands on her table, she's inserted under the glass a little snap of Tam sitting in Catherine's pushchair, dressed in a red hood. He hated every minute of it. I was there when Catherine dressed him up and he simply wouldn't stay still.

Tam himself never buried or hoarded things—they always had to be in use. A real artist in this.

*   *   *

Marianne only mentions Tam at odd moments, as he comes to mind, associated with places in the house or garden or along the street, shared activities, mealtimes especially. Then she goes quiet.

They say you can tell a man by the company he keeps. I'd choose Tam any day!

TUESDAY, 18 JANUARY

Over lunch in the Staff Club, a colleague, when told about Tam's death, and how we buried him, said
"Are you quite sure he was dead?"
I couldn't help thinking of the story about a lecturer in theology dying suddenly one evening while watching television. On being told, his professor's first words:
"And what was the programme?"

WEDNESDAY, 19 JANUARY

Today I went to J. Kinghorn, the photographer, along Marchmont Road to get enlargements made of the best photographs of Tam. They'll be some sort of record.

SATURDAY, 22 JANUARY

Director of Finance
City Chambers,
High Street,
EDINBURGH EH1 1YP

Dear Sir
Thank you for your card of 31st December 1976, reminding us that our dog's licence expires on that date. I write to inform you that our dog, Tam, was killed in a road accident on 3rd January 1977.

Yours sincerely
Derek Bowman

WEDNESDAY, 26 JANUARY

Marianne has been hoovering the floor. The wire rattled slightly just now against the door of the living-room. I immediately thought, that's "the boy", leaning his weight forward against the door, to push it open and rush in to join me here at the table. First that scratching, then a black wet nose, then in no time at all him jumping up.

TUESDAY, 1 FEBRUARY

Whenever we went up Midmar Avenue to the allotments, how he'd flatten with anticipation! I can still feel the pull, the tug of excitement, right up the lead to the palm of my hand.

Or he'd seek to draw my hand from whatever book I was reading to stroke his head.

THURSDAY, 10 FEBRUARY

Elisabeth's bought herself a new Diana Ross record which she's been playing a lot. She's becoming very fond of music, I've noticed.

Tonight, when I went up to say goodnight to the girls—they were sleeping together, head to toe—Elisabeth started making hints about getting a new dog. I said we must mourn Tam for a decent space of time, there must be none of the "off with the old, on with the new" attitude. "He wasn't simply a pair of gloves," I said.

TUESDAY, 15 FEBRUARY

Tonight I was doing the washing-up in the kitchen with Catherine— she's been very helpful lately—and as we came to the last of the dishes, I found half a wooden peg in the plastic rack on the draining-board. It was soaked through. Catherine said, "I bet Tam got the other half!"

WEDNESDAY, 16 FEBRUARY

One of the few times I dirtied my hands stroking Tam was after he was run over. And that was no fault of his. The road was wet.

SUNDAY, 20 FEBRUARY

"Here, Dad, here's your tea!" shouts Catherine from the kitchen, and through her words I can hear the exact intonation of "Here, Tam, come and get your tea!"

First he'd rush to the door of the front room, stand there for me to open it, then released, dash to the kitchen to lap up his favourite beverage. He did everything keenly, like a small child. Have you ever seen these toddlers out with their young parents, importantly pushing their pushchairs (their handles so much taller than themselves) or waddling away, being naughty, their fat legs full of creases, only to plump down on their amply padded rubber-knickered bottoms? All great fun.

Yes, like a child he was. Eager, too eager. It doesn't do.

WEDNESDAY, 23 FEBRUARY

Before I went up to bed last night I checked that the gas and electricity were off downstairs and the doors properly locked. Instinctively I found myself looking into the dark kitchen to see if Tam was safely ensconced in his box. Then the usual pang.

TUESDAY, 1 MARCH

That neighbour who, when I was so ill-advised as to express my concern that I might have pruned our willow-tree too severely, said
"Aye, you're quite right to be worried, dear. You know what you've done? Cut its veins—that's what. It'll bleed to death!"

SATURDAY, 12 MARCH

Marianne hoovering after breakfast. The hall's flooded with light, streaming in through the "broad-reeded" glass of the front door.
She stops in her tracks, switches off and says,
"Derek, do you see anything?"
"Where?"
"There, under the chair."
"Can't say I do."
"Bend down and look properly."
"Only a lightish patch in the carpet."
"Exactly, you know what it's from? From Tam, that's where he used to lie." (Yes, latterly it had become a favourite bed of his). "It's the grease in his coat that did it."
"Of course."
Then for some reason I thought of sunlight blanching a bookcover, only with that, the book loses value—at least in the eyes of the dealer it does.

SUNDAY, 13 MARCH

There's a ghastly, brisk little man in a pork-pie hat, armed with secateurs, clipping off any new buds that have dared to appear on the trees opposite. He cut them back viciously last year, ruined what were four beautiful ash-trees growing by the tennis pavilion.
How do you contain these spoilers?

SUNDAY, 20 MARCH

If only I'd shown more sense of responsibility. After all *I'm* the adult, I'm supposed to be the one with experience. Catherine's still only a child, twelve is no age. I should have warned her. Of course it's sobered her, she's quietened down, is no longer so childish. But what a dreadful way for us to learn our lesson!—when it's too late.

MONDAY, 21 MARCH

As Marianne and I were washing the tea-things just now I happened to throw out a cheese-rind, remarking
"He'd have loved this."
"Yes," said Marianne, "Do you know? I thought he was there last Saturday when we had the Rentons in for dinner."
"How?"
"As we were all settling down in the front room for coffee, Bob lifted his black shoe, the way you do, placing one leg over another. For a moment I thought it's Tam jumping up—that black shoe. I very nearly shouted 'Get down, Tam!' Out of sheer habit."

TUESDAY, 22 MARCH

Term finished last Friday. Glad to have a bit of time to catch up on myself. This morning I went shopping into Morningside by myself. This afternoon as I sit here in the front room reading, I think of Tam lying warm against my feet.

WEDNESDAY, 23 MARCH

While we were watching the table-tennis tournament on the television—all those sharp little Asians beating the socks off us Europeans—Marianne said "Do you remember, Derek, the way Tam used to sit there on that patch behind the wire-netting, watching the tennis?"
"Tethered", I answered.
"Of course".

FRIDAY, 2 MARCH

Yesterday afternoon the sun had a bit of heat in it. At last! It's been a hard winter.
When I got home I first watered the house-plants in the porch and the

front room, then, having walked round "the estate" at the front, admiring the fresh shoots coming up everywhere, I trained the two clematises growing up the trellis between our porch and the bay-window. Then, for the first time since Tam died, I ventured down to the apple-trees by the railway. For a moment I stood at his grave, where a few daffodils and bluebells were coming up under the trees.

As I walked back up to the house I was gladdened to see that the little pear-tree we put in last year has taken. We'd had our doubts.

MONDAY, 28 MARCH

If we were enjoying ourselves, wouldn't he join in! But if one or other of us in the house had a row or there were people having words on the television, then Tam would get so upset. He'd get up, wander about restlessly, finally seeking refuge under the sideboard where, lying prone, his eyes would roam the room, looking from one person to another for an easing of the situation. Or else he'd stand at the living-room door (it opened inwards so he couldn't lean on it and push it open), asking to be let out into the kitchen where, after a few turns, he'd slowly nestle down with a sigh into his box—"These human beings!"

WEDNESDAY, 30 MARCH

Blowy. This afternoon I was helping Marianne get the washing in— all those sun-showers!

I looked down.

"What are those bits of stuff" I said, "lying about the lawn? Do you think they're from cats?"

"No, they're from Tam. The dung's been all washed away by now by rain and snow and frost. General wear and tear."

And there they were—navy-blue, red, green—according to what material he'd eaten. Washed clean.

What a job we had getting the girls to clear up the lawns!

Then I remembered the sheep and cow-dung lying about the fields and on the concrete path to the camp on Iona where I stayed last June. Bright sun, grey clouds—that strange light.

THURSDAY, 31 MARCH

Yesterday, out walking, I noticed how badly bashed the railings were on the corner of Morningside Road and Cluny Gardens. Some crash during the night, no doubt. The garden wall along Oswald Road, knocked down a few weeks ago, has now been repaired. Violence now displayed, now hidden, always lurking.

The number of windows that were wantonly shattered every week-end round Forrest Road where we lived for seven years. One Saturday night someone spat on the windscreen of our car parked along there, and regularly the drunks used to come and foul the hallway of our common stair. They didn't sing, they shouted about the streets. Someone even took Catherine's mattress out of her pram, parked in our hall, and pissed all over it. Again and again those beautiful flowering cherry saplings, planted so carefully across the Meadows, were ruined by vandals.

Tam pushing his small black head against my hand, while I read. Needing tenderness.

Human beings. Animals.

FRIDAY, 1 APRIL

Today, April Fool's Day, a good 16 or 17 years ago, I caned two lads. That was during my seven years as schoolmaster (a good biblical number). Well, lads can take things too far. I had my livelihood to consider. Now I have other problems than discipline. Why am I writing this? Out of a sense of guilt? Grief? Which is predominant?

I should have been stricter. With Tam, I mean.

*   *   *

As we were sitting reading in the living-room this evening, Marianne said,

"At least the only damage he did was to himself."

"Tam, you mean?"

"Yes, I was afraid he might have caused a serious accident."

"I suppose so."

"And he wasn't mangled or left a cripple."

"There is that consolation."

"His death was a clean break" she finished decisively.

—But is any bereavement a *clean* break?

SATURDAY, 2 APRIL

How light he was at first!—like a bird. Nothing to him inside that black woolliness of his, fluffing in the wind, when you gathered him up in your arms and hugged him. And so warm, with his eager heart going twenty to the dozen!

SUNDAY, 3 APRIL

Yesterday I read a review of a book, entitled "Life As We Have Known It", by Cooperative Working Women:
    "Mrs Burrow, at the age of eight, was the oldest in a gang of children put to work 14 hours a day in the fenland fields followed 'by an old man carrying a long whip in his hand which he did not forget to use'. When, later, she saw the real countryside, the delight of her life was 'to watch the larks rise up out of the cornfield singing as if their throats would burst'."
That's exactly what I felt with Tam out in the open, the pure gladness.

MONDAY, 4 APRIL

Our willow-tree is blossoming!—innumerable fat yellow catkins all over. I've never seen it so beautiful. So much pollen it covers your hands.

As children, we'd hold buttercups under each others' chins, "Do you like butter?", and see the yellow reflected. Yellow as the colour of spring—daffodils, forsythia, willow. Like the sun itself, the great healer.

The bright-faced yellow coltsfoot I picked by the allotments last week, now standing in the little vase on my table, have already grown two inches since I brought them indoors. I see them thriving on tips, builders' yards, old quarries. Waste ground generally.

Good for wounds—so they say.